www.TheHummingbirdReview.com

volume II, number 1                    spring 2011

Published by Open Books Press, USA
www.openbookspress.com

*The Hummingbird Review* presents fine writing by both new writers and fully established literary figures. The review is committed to portraying the beauty and challenges of life – the full human experience – through literature and art, and promotes cross-cultural writing in all forms.

**Publisher/Executive Editor:**
Charles Redner

**Editor:**
Robert Yehling

**Associate Editors:**
Said Leghlid
Elia Esparza

**Editorial Intern:**
Madison Kawakami

**Permissions:**
"Eagle Poem," from *How We Become Human: New and Selected Poems*, Joy Harjo (Norton: 1975-2001) by permission of the author.
"Back On The Bowery 45 Years Later: Poetry and All That Jazz," David Amram by permission of the author.
Lyrics: "Leon Came Back," Gary Lawless, by permission of the author.
"In The Trees," Michael Blake, excerpt from forthcoming book, *Into The Stars,* by permission of the author.
"The Uninvited Guest," Wm Thompson Ong, excerpt from forthcoming book, *The Lake*, by permission of the author.
Excerpt from *Tales From The Eastside: The Stories That Never Get Told,* Isaac Lomeli by permission of the author.
"For Neal Cassady on his birthday," David Amram by permission of the author.
Portions of "Earth Verse," "Prayer for the Great Family," "Axe Handles," "How Poetry Comes to Me" and "Finding the Space in the Heart" appear in "Morning Tea with Gary Snyder" by permission of Gary Snyder.

Cover painting by Judith DiGirolamo Redner, www.jdiart.com
Book and cover design by Open Books Press
© 2011 Charles J. Redner

ISBN: 978-0-9846359-1-7

This book is printed on acid free paper.
Printed in the USA

# Eagle Poem

To pray you open your whole self
To sky, to earth, to sun, to moon
To one whole voice that is you.
And know there is more
That you can't see, can't hear
Can't know except in moments
Steadily growing, and in languages
That aren't always sound but other
Circles of motion.
Like eagle that Sunday morning
Over Salt River.  Circles in blue sky
In wind, swept our hearts clean
With sacred wings.
We see you, see ourselves and know
That we must take the utmost care
And kindness in all things.
Breathe in, knowing we are made of
All this, and breathe, knowing
We are truly blessed because we
Were born, and die soon, within a
True circle of motion,
Like eagle rounding out the morning
Inside us.
We pray that it will be done
In beauty.
In beauty.

# TABLE OF CONTENTS
Vol. II, No. 1 • spring 2011

**CHARLES REDNER**

## Publisher's statement
# Sing Praise for the Words!

Muse, please do not fail me now.

I begin each issue with "Sing praise for the words." Don't believe there is a more appropriate oath for this labor of love we named, *The Hummingbird Review*. To wit, the issue you now hold, shines a laser-lamp on one of the most electrifying, dramatic and fruitful ages in American literature, proclaimed the "Beat Generation" by other than the exceptional writers who lived it. Read the reflections of a few octogenarians who participated. We bring you a glimpse of the energy field that they generated.

Overhear Jack Kerouac talking with David Amram. Follow Gary Snyder as he walks through six decades of poetry at his Kitkitdizze home. Another clan member, poet Gary Lawless, chips in with lyrics reminiscent of a tale from the Korean or Vietnam Wars – although it would be apropos for any conflict. Among those learning from the West Coast Beats in Berkeley was Kate Harding, who shares the experience in one of her three poems this issue.

Alone with me in the basement of a New Jersey motor lodge, a presidential candidate who vigorously campaigned against the Vietnam War took off his suit coat. Two secret service agents remained stationed at the top of the stairs. He unbuttoned and removed his shirt, unbuckled his belt, stripped to his shorts and handed me each article of clothing as he dressed in more "conservative" attire. He explained that he was heading to New York City and didn't want the folks back in South Dakota, via national television coverage, to see how he appeared during the luncheon stump-speech delivered minutes earlier.

Now I possessed the answer to *the* burning question of the '72 campaign, asked by at least one reporter at each stop. The candidate glared at me and said, "Charlie, swear—swear you'll never give the answer to the boxers or briefs question."

"Yes, Senator, I promise." But I wondered if travelling campaign reporter, Hunter S. (Gonzo) Thompson, if he knew, would keep Sen. George McGovern's deepest personal secret. I imagined not.

I retell this incident now because Thompson was greatly influenced by the "Beat Generation" writers. He counted William Burroughs and Allen Ginsberg among his circle of friends. Of the nearly three hundred who attended Thompson's funeral in 2005, George McGovern was there to bid farewell to his old friend. Hope you enjoy our look back at these mid-20th century writers who carved out a special place for themselves in American literature.

I suggest you start with "Morning Tea with Gary Snyder" by our editor, Bob Yehling, himself a decades-long student of Beat literature. (To note: Bob dipped into the nurturing force of the Beat literature movement, City Lights Books in San Francisco, on this past Christmas Eve, to buy a copy of the first scroll/draft of Kerouac's *On The Road.)*

Can you say *Novels 'R' Us?* Academy Award writer Michael Blake graciously sends us an exclusive chapter from his new novella, *Into The Stars.* Set in World War I, Michael finds a way to tell a love story of a man for a horse. Newcomer William Thompson Ong shares a chapter from *The Lake*, his soon to be published historical drama set against the backdrop of a great American tragedy, the Johnstown Flood of May 31, 1889.

We have been blessed by so many brilliant writers who have graciously provided us with their work. It constantly amazes me how generous these renowned contributors are with their time and their writings. This time around, National Book Award nominee Harvey Stanbrough presents us with a short story, along with a few poems.

Continuing with our multicultural offerings in every issue, we feature Native-American Joy Harjo, Mexican-American Isaac Lomeli, and Chinese-American Mai Lon Gittelsohn. The September 2010 Southern California Writers' Conference contest winner, E. Scott Menter, shares his poignant title, "Dolphinarium." Some twenty writers fill out our line-up with an incredible variety of amazing poems.

Our goal is to share the words of established writers while, at the same time, reach out to help new writers who may someday become the "Beat Generation" of their day.

Charles Redner, publisher

profile

**ROBERT YEHLING**

# Morning Tea with Gary Snyder

*Wide enough to keep you looking*
*Open enough to keep you moving*
*Dry enough to keep you honest*
*Prickly enough to make you tough*
*Green enough to go on living*
*Old enough to give you dreams[1]*

The walk down the hill is a ritual of its own. Sun-streaked ponderosa pines wave in the Sierra breeze. Manzanita guards a hardpack road of decomposed granite and red clay, softened by overnight rain, which breaks into two paths. To the right lies a Zendo where people have come to sit in *zazen* for four decades. To the left stands a low-lying house with a distinct Japanese flavor to its layout, a Native American sense of connectedness to earth, each square foot serving and feeding the entire home, created by one man's vision and no power tools. It sits on a tucked-in piece of land that, for forty years, has borne a name that represents so much in literary, environmental and conservation circles: *Kitkitdizze*.

Gary Snyder stands outside near several cords of meticulously stacked firewood. Emmy, a German water dog with razor-sharp awareness (like her owner), runs out and checks the guest. She maps with her nose: "She always sniffs everything, then re-sniffs it next time to see what's familiar, what's new — and records it," Gary says. I'm getting re-sniffed; she jumps up to be petted. Decked in a heavy sweater, Gary's full head of white hair, beard, half-tired eyes and lined, leathered face give him the look of a salty ship captain or mountain man, his face a roadmap of depth, serenity, battles mostly won. A sage's face. He faces the east, which should come as no surprise, since he's been sharing and translating the literary and deeper cultural treasures and wisdoms of the east with Turtle Island, North America for more than a half-century.

"Good morning." He offers a hand that has acted on behalf of its owner to build lookouts, shovel coal into ship boilers, saw and chop wood, tend gardens, grab onto craggy mountain peaks and deep Pleistocene caves, fight battles to preserve and conserve home and place, and write thousands of poems and essays built to live forever. His handshake resonates with a life and a mind so rich, purposeful and meaningful to others that, to commemorate his 60th birthday, friends, acquaintances and colleagues created a Snyder tribute anthology, *Dimensions of a Life*, one of the best studies of a living writer ever published. It seems he's been even busier in the 20 years since *Dimensions* came out.

Hearing a loud, sonorous tone up the hill, Gary turns toward his immediate neighbor, the Ananda meditation retreat and its tiny College of Living Wisdom. He bought Kitkitdizze in 1967 in a four-way land purchase-and-divide with the founder of Ananda, Swami Kriyananda, as well as fellow poet Allen Ginsberg and San Francisco Zen Center leader Richard "Roshi" Baker. "What does that bell signify?" he asks, his voice as deep as the bell.

"It's the second bell of the morning. It comes at the end of meditation, but it's the call to breakfast," I reply.

He nods, studying me like an eagle. Gary is always studying with his eyes, ears, senses. It makes hanging out with him an even more remarkable experience. "Let's go inside, make some tea and talk about some writing and everything else that's going on."

We walk to the back deck of his house, which opens to his bedroom. Before walking in, he points to a barn about forty feet away. "That's my summer office, where I keep all my books, where I write. Got all sorts of things in there. I just don't use it in the winter. Too damned cold."

As he talks, I sink into the meaning of his words, how much Gary Snyder personally means to me. These are deep, deep roots; I've sat across the road (and on back stretches of Kitkitdizze, surreptitiously) in meditation many times in the past 25 years. I've written some of my favorite poems while straddling his land. His poetic and narrative collections have influenced my writing to the bone: *Turtle Island, No Nature, Practice of the Wild, Into the Fire, A Place In Space, Axe Handles,* and the masterpiece he took 40 years to complete, *Mountains and Rivers Without End.* Like thousands of other college students in the mid- and late-1970s, I picked up *Turtle Island,* became enthralled in how Gary cut to the chase every time, took the "pledge of allegiance to Turtle Island"[2], and fused my soul to the sublime "Prayer for the Great Family," seven perfect Mohawk-influenced stanzas (to Mother Earth, Plants, Air, Wild Beings, Water, Sun and Great Sky) that closes with:

> *Gratitude to the Great Sky*
> *   who holds billions of stars — and goes yet beyond that —*
> *   beyond all powers, and thoughts*
> *   and yet is within us —*
> *   Grandfather Space.*
> *   The Mind is his Wife.*

so be it.[3]

While inhaling the brisk, pine-sharpened air of the surrounding Animin Forest along the San Juan Ridge, high above the South Yuba River, I consider the facets of Gary Snyder: poetics, ecology, Native American myth and literature, the value of work, Japanese and Chinese poetry. The San Francisco Beat movement. That ignited the October night in 1955 when Gary joined Ginsberg, Michael McClure, Kenneth Rexroth, Philip Whalen, Philip Lamantia and their non-reading guest, Jack Kerouac, at the "remarkable collection of angels," the Six Gallery Reading Ginsberg debuted and immortalized "Howl." Snyder, then 25, read his first poem publicly, "A Berry Feast," now a classic. The Six Gallery remains the seminal poetry event in recent U.S. history — and for which, amazingly, no photograph or tape recording exists. Why? No one thought it was a big deal. They didn't see what was coming. Except for the lookout, the erstwhile Cascade Mountain ranger and U.C. Berkeley graduate student, Snyder. "I think it will be a poetical bombshell," he told Whalen. In a journal, he wrote, "Poetry will get a kick in the arse around this town."[4]

All of them became famous.

A few nights before, while having dinner, Gary and I talked about Kerouac. After the Six Gallery reading, and before heading to Japan for 12 years of study, Snyder took Kerouac up North Arete, a.k.a. the Sierra Matterhorn, a difficult six-hour climb just west of California's Mt. Whitney. The two held a common devotion for Buddhism, but were otherwise as different as the West and East coasts from which they came. Not to mention that Kerouac wrote prose that sometimes rambled like an endless river (one particular sentence in his benzedrine-fueled novel, *The Subterraneans,* stretched more than 1,200 words). Conversely, Snyder lives and breathes punctuality, his work crisp and clear as cold, pine-scented air. In 1959, their Sierra Matterhorn climb appeared in Kerouac's great novel, *The Dharma Bums* — along with a wise, resourceful protagonist virtually every reader before and since wanted to know like a next-door neighbor: Japhy Ryder.

*Gary Snyder.* "That was interesting to see how he wrote about our trip, the things we did together," Gary said. "He had a tough time getting up the Matterhorn, but he did it."

"What's it like becoming the protagonist of a novel?"

Gary looked at me, eyes sharpening to the point he was about to make. His next bite of food clung to his fork like a spacewalker. "I was the *model* for a fictional character. I'm no more Japhy Ryder than the next guy. He used a lot of what we did, and I liked the way he wrote the book very much — I think it's Kerouac's finest novel — but Japhy is fictional and I'm right here. I was just a model."

An intriguing comment I read about Kerouac's work came to mind, something relevant in this era of memoirs, exposés, autobiographical novels, what's true in novels and what's fictional in so-called memoirs. "Do you think that if Kerouac were alive today, his thirteen novels — *On The Road, Dharma Bums, Big Sur, Tales of Duluoz* and the others — would be considered memoirs?" I asked.

Gary thought about it for a moment, leaving the food marooned. He shook the fork slightly. "That's a very good question. But... no. He fictionalized quite a bit, changed some names, changed the sequence of events, made a couple of things up; it's not true memoir. You could call it autobiographical fiction. But why not just call it fiction and enjoy it?"

Out rolled the raucous laugh, the fun-lover's laugh, his eyes jovial as leprechauns — the side of Gary Snyder we all seem to forget while he's reading his works and discoursing on everything from the dearth of deep thought in everyday life to instilling more arts into public education to conserving his beloved Sierra Nevada. When you hear people on the San Juan Ridge talk about him, they say the same thing: *I wouldn't want to be on his bad side.* The U.S. Department of Interior and Bureau of Land Management know all about that; Snyder is not only, according to many including the *Los Angeles Times,* "the greatest nature poet alive," but also the greatest protector of the Sierra since John Muir. He might be a Buddhist, but threaten to exploit the Sierra or anything or anyone else near and dear to him, and his serenity will transform into the roar of a ferocious, five-foot, five-inch tiger.

Gary remains as much a student of nature and life now as he was at Reed College 60 years ago. This man with an encyclopedic memory, razor-sharp wit, eagle's alertness, astute knowledge of the land and the skill to write some of the most celebrated literary works in print always seeks to learn more. Whether conversing with folks at the nearby Mother Trucker's natural foods market about the rare MacNabb Cypress, haggling with the U.S. Forestry Service over ways to prevent the next big fire from wiping out the San Juan Ridge, or discoursing with intellectuals at a panel discussion, he is the eager student who raises his hand over and over again and keeps asking the right questions. Then he sits — still as a lunar night — and listens while absorbing every bit of the non-verbal information that passes by. That degree of presence is why a single Gary Snyder poem can carry a physical observation, a teaching, an animal or plant's language, a kernel of geologic history, a Chinese, Native American or Japanese literary citing, a human relationship with the moment — or environment — and a Buddhist or indigenous edge carved into the side. Or burned into your consciousness. He always blows the conch shell, like he did at San Francisco's Golden Gate Park in January 1967 to call the Human Be-In to order. Our job is to put everything aside and step into his place for a few words.

*And I say this to Kai*
*"Look: We shape the handle*
*By checking the handle*
*Of the axe we cut with—"*
*And he sees. And I hear it again:*
*It's in Lu Ji's We Fu, fourth century*
*A.D. "Essay on Literature" — in the*
*Preface: "In making the handle*
*Of an axe*
*By cutting wood with an axe*
*The model is indeed near at hand."*
*My teacher Shih-hsiang Chen*
*Translated that and taught it years ago*
*And I see: Pound was an axe,*
*Chen was an axe, I am an axe*
*And my son a handle, soon*
*To be shaping again, model*
*And tool, craft of culture,*
*How we go on.*[5]

A fun cross-reading experience is to mix vernacular Chinese literary-wanderer novels such as *The Travels of Lao Ts'an* with Gary's remarkable essays " 'Wild' in China," "Walls Within Walls" and "The Brush."[6] These pieces weave poetry, literature, brush painting and the integral role of the wandering citizen-poet into works of narrative art. Gary writes from experience: he's wandered tens of thousands of miles along the Pacific Rim alone. He's also one of the best American translators of classic Chinese poetry. Why source watered-down textbook histories when you can *move* and *breathe* through the wandering poets' souls thanks to the way Gary has recounted journeys and translated poets like Han Shan (9th century, *Cold Mountain Poems)* and Wang-Wei (8th century)? He even translated a short poem from an 18-year-old homeless Mongolian boy — the future warrior Jenghiz (Genghis) Khan. "They helped me to 'see' fields, farms, tangles of brush, the azaleas in the back of an old brick apartment," he wrote. "They freed me from excessive attachment to wild mountains, with their way of suggesting that even the wildest hills are places where people, also, live."[7]

Therein lies perhaps Gary's greatest teaching, the root of his poems and Kitkitdizze: *Know thy home. Know thy place.* He lives by the moral compass of the ancient Greek saying *oikos nomos* — "managing the household." *Oikos* is the root word of "ecology." As one of his book titles states, Gary's household is *Earth Household.* "If you know about the household, you know about the watershed," he told *The Paris Review.*

"Once you learn about the place you're in, you can learn about yourself," he says. "That was the basis of a lot of my writing instruction at U.C. Davis." Take his translation of a Wang-Wei poem:

> *Empty mountains:*
>> *no one to be seen,*
> *Yet—hear—*
>> *human sounds and echoes.*
> *Returning sunlight*
>> *enters the dark woods;*
> *Again shining*
>> *on green moss, above.*[8]

Gary sits on the desk chair of his cozy winter office, which looks out to his backyard and the sugar and Ponderosa pines beyond. The ever-loving, assertive Emmy lavishes her attention and affection on me. "You're new to her; you're young, fun and exciting," Gary says. "I think she's getting bored of being around me all the time. Would you like some tea?"

Gary ambles into the kitchen and brews tea. His back area is as efficient and multi-purpose as a single-room dwelling in the Nepalese highlands. On the far side stands his bed, head facing west, a thanga of the Blue Healing Buddha on the wall. Photos and mementos from a few of his travels perch on walls and shelves. Books flock everywhere. Titles include Chinese literary commentary, country living, California and Mexican nature and wildlife, natural histories of the surrounding mountains, various poetry collections from Wordsworth to Basho, and one of R.H. Blyth's seminal haiku volumes.

He returns with a small kettle of green tea. He sits the platter on the low-lying coffee table. There are three filled Japanese teacups on the platter, intentionally positioned; the third faces west, towards the setting sun, towards the portrait of Gary's beloved wife, Carole Koda. She's still present in the room, four years after succumbing to cancer, her spirit joining us for morning tea.

For a few minutes, we don't speak. No need to.

As Gary sips, he points to a table on which sits three of my books, including *Shades of Green.* "Your work is interesting," he says. "Good use of imagery and emotion. Nice observations. Very diverse."

*Fourteen words I will cherish forever.* I thank him.

"Who worked with you when you started out?" he asks.

"Don Eulert, down at the old U.S. International in San Diego. He was the founding editor of *American Haiku* magazine in the '60s."

Gary smiles and nods his head. An impish memory curls in his eyes. "Don Eulert — now there's a poet. One of the few people who really knows and understand haiku. I remember a reading I did for his students down there in San Diego — Ocean Beach, 1973. I remember everyone was ... *happy.*" He laughs. "Show me something he taught you that you've passed along to your students."

One day in 1979, Don told me to come up with 25 "power words" that resonated within my being whenever I said or wrote them. A partial list: *deer, sun, ocean, wave, star, eye, cascade, eagle, run.* He then said to write one word apiece on an index card. Next time I saw him, we played five-card draw with my power words. "Now arrange the five words into an image. Then write a poem or vignette from that image," Don said.

Don's power word card deck is an ideal way for writers to acquaint themselves with their own power words and core images. "I like that, a lot," Gary says. "Don Eulert is a very wise man, in tune with every word he writes."

A few months later, before an enthralled crowd, Don wore a coyote pelt over his head and read a couple of stanzas from Gary's poem "A Berry Feast," along with a coyote poem of his own at *The Hummingbird Review Poetry Revue* group. Among the listeners: *Dances With Wolves* author Michael Blake. As Gary would say, "the old ways": returning the compliment without a prompting word spoken. No need to.

We talk for almost an hour about haiku, tanga, reng-kyu, shih, and other short-line Japanese and Chinese poetry. We open with Don's book, *Field,* a collection of 365 haiku he wrote during a calendar year, one-a-day style, from his Frog Farm spread in eastern San Diego County. Only one person meant more than Don to haiku's emergence in America — and it wasn't Gary, much as people credit him because of his translations, friendship with Japanese wandering poet Nanao Sakaki, and deep roots in Japanese culture and poetry. It was Reginald Horace (R.H.) Blyth (1898-1964), who fell in love with Japan in the mid-1920s, later tutored Crown Prince (and future Emperor) Akihito, and introduced the world to a precious poetic form with his seminal four-volume work, *Haiku.*

"A haiku is not a poem, it is not literature; it is a hand beckoning, a door half-opened, a mirror wiped clean,"[9] Gary says, quoting Blyth from memory while looking out the window. He turns and peers at me, his eyes steeling, the precisionist rising. "What it is *not* is contrived lines of 5-7-5 syllables. First of all, Japanese doesn't translate to English like that. Second, haiku is an expression, a movement — like Blyth said, 'the expression of a temporary enlightenment in which we see into the life of things.' I think people get too caught up in form — why can't we just focus on listening, observing and writing good poetry?"

His passionate argument reminded me of "How Poetry Comes to Me," about the most solid tutorial we're going to find in six lines:

> *It comes blundering over the*
> *Boulders at night, it stays*
> *Frightened outside the*
> *Range of my campfire*
> *I go to meet it at the*
> *Edge of the light*[10]

A few days prior, Gary addressed the Ananda College of Living Wisdom students. He showed up three weeks after his 80th birthday for a reading, but he had another message in mind: talk to the students about forming relationship with place, *this* place, this neck of the San Juan Ridge on which they matriculated. *Oikos nomos.* "Gary's work presents a lifestyle of relationship to the place where you're living: practicing compassion and *ahimsa* towards all sentient beings; embracing and *living* within the ecology of the land; always learning and being open-minded; attuning through meditation; and learning from our human ancestors – a 50,000-year family tree, far as he's concerned," I said in an introductory talk. "We're here for a purpose, to co-exist with the planet, not to dominate it. The land will be here long after we depart; let's add to its sustenance and learn everything we can about its ecology and history, its magic and mystery ('when there are mountains and rivers, there are spirits,' he writes), know our neighbors, attune to our particular paths, and serve the light and all beings. Each other included.

"Once upon a time, when the Maidu, Mono, Nisenan and Sierra Miwok peoples lived here, long before the four Johns – Sutter, Donner, Powell and Muir – traversed these mountains, these were considered normal values and ethics. Now, because of the way things have gone, we call them 'alternative.' We've forgotten the old ways; Gary has re-introduced them to a wide audience."

For the next 45 minutes, students and faculty alike were enthralled. From rote memory, Gary painted the 300-million year history of where we sat, the cataclysms, mountain ranges birthing and oceans dying, rivers switching directions and foothills calving, wise use of resources by the Natives, the San Joaquin's pre-agricultural status as a lush bird tule swamp nirvana, and the shifts that led to Northern California's wet winters and hot, dry summers (shared by only four other regions: the Mediterranean, Chilean coast, South Africa and Australia's Gold Coast). With a professor's knowledge and a storyteller's way of captivating audiences, Gary brush-painted the history of the San Juan Ridge — a biological anomaly where the south-facing plant life stretches to Mexico, while the north-facing plants life extends into Canada. He talked about working with the habitat, citizen responsibilities, and the simple value of walking the trails, learning about place ... learning about self. It brought to mind one of many titles assigned to Gary over the years (some he likes, others he doesn't): *The poet laureate of deep ecology.* The hills, four-leggeds and trees bestowed that title upon him as much as any human.

Gary talked about the first white man to appreciate California's treasures, John Wesley Powell: "He wanted to re-draw the California state line because he hated how its natural geological boundaries were ignored in the haste of its addition to the Union," Gary explained. He finished his talk by reading from *No Nature,* his 1992 collection. "When I'm talking about place, and I say 'here,' I mean 'right here.'" He pointed to the ground. Then he read another four poems from *No Nature,* including his personal favorite, "Right in the Trail."

He smiled. Mischievously. He held a handwritten letter from a 13-year-old girl he'd met during a talk at the nearby North Columbia School. The girl, who recently moved away, wrote him a letter — in rhyme. A rhyming Gary Snyder poem is rare as a California condor.

Gary read his response. It closed with,

> *"And you've gotten some rhyme out of this writer/*
> *Gary Snyder"*

At 80, Gary continues to work and read at a clip that would make many full-time workers hyperventilate. "The thing I hate about being 80 is that I don't have any choice now; I have to slow down. My body's making me do it," he says. *Slow down...* Gary had just finished three months of college readings from Virginia to Portland, culminating with the 30th anniversary commemoration of the Mount Saint Helen's eruption. Gary's dance with Mount Saint Helen's stretches back decades before the mountain blew itself in half; in 1945, it was the first Cascade peak Gary summited. He was 15. He holds her near and dear.

On the right side of Gary's desk, on a single index card taped to a single plastic in-box, are the words: "Today's Work."

What about today's work? "I'm really busy right now," he said, his eyes flashing in profound love of the process. "I'm writing two books, one about building this house by hand, the other about my wife's people." He shares a few threads of the narratives, which will be available for all to see in the near future.

The man will not rest easily. His energy truly is indefatigable. What a blessing for the rest of us.

I stand up and extend my hand. As we shake, he says, "I really appreciate you giving me your books."

"Well, I have just about everything you've written — an entire shelf. Plus a broadside of 'A Berry Feast,' *Dimensions of a Life,* and all sorts of other things." I paused. "I think it's always nice for teachers to see the way the inspire and seed the work of others, how their efforts are played forward."

His eyes sparkle as he smiles. "Do you have this one?" He hands me a hardback copy of *The Gary Snyder Reader*. Then he signs it, with a cherry on top:

29 • V • 2010
Kitkitdizze

As I walk down his driveway, I rub my thumb on the muddy earth. I smudge the frontispiece of the book, marking my place in his space on this day.

*The space goes on.*
*But the wet black brush*
*tip draws to a point,*
*lifts away.*[11]

REFERENCES:

1. "Earth Verse," from *Mountains and Rivers Without End,* by Gary Snyder.
2. "I pledge allegiance to the soil/of Turtle Island/and to the begins who thereon dwell/one ecosystem/in diversity/under the sun/with joyful interpenetration for all."
3. From *Turtle Island,* (1974: North Point Press), winner of the 1975 Pulitzer Prize for Poetry.
4. From "When The Beats Came Back," feature story, *Reed Magazine,* Winter 2008. Gary Snyder earned his bachelor's degree at Reed College in Portland, then and now one of the finest and most stringent liberal arts institutions in the U.S.
5. From "Axe Handles," *Axe Handles* (2005: Counterpoint)
6. "'Wild' in China," "Walls Within Walls" and "The Brush" are essays from "The Great Clod" Project, unpublished in collection form until released in 2000 in *The Gary Snyder Reader.*
7. "'Wild' in China."
8. ibid.
9. From Blyth, R.W., *Haiku, 1949-52: Volume 1: Eastern Culture* (The Hokuseido Press), p. 243. The full quote: "A haiku is not a poem, it is not literature; it is a hand becoming, a door half-opened, a mirror wiped clean. It is a way of returning to nature, to our moon nature, our cherry blossom nature, our falling leaf nature, in short, to our Buddha nature. It is a way in which the cold winter rain, the swallows of evening, even the every day in its hotness, and the length of the night, become truly alive, share in our humanity, speak their own silent and expressive language."
10. "How Poetry Comes to Me," from *No Nature* (1993: Pantheon)
11. From "Finding the Space in the Heart," *Mountains and Rivers Without End* (1997: Counterpoint)

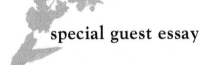 special guest essay

**DAVID AMRAM**

# Back on the Bowery 45 Years Later:
## POETRY AND ALL THAT JAZZ

Editor's Note:

*Composer and jazz musician David Amram, a major participant and driving force in the New York Beat scene of the 1950s, wrote this piece in 2002, on the occasion of the Bowery Poetry Club's opening.*

I rarely play clubs anymore. However, earlier in the decade, I was asked to do so by four different people, including Levi Asher, founder of LitKicks, at four different events at the Bowery Poetry Club during a six-week period. All four of the poets who contacted me, while different from one another, have a common connection to the tradition that Jack Kerouac and I, along with poets Howard Hart and Philip Lamantia, pioneered at the first-ever jazz poetry reading given in NYC, in October 1957 at the Brata Art Gallery.

Unbeknownst to us, it started what became a fad (usually a sure step towards mediocrity and doom), called "Jazz/Poetry." All this died a natural death a short time later, when readers and musicians, thrown together without an understanding they could collaborate and create their own magic, instead were told that they had to compete to see who could drown out each other first.

Still, the seeds had been sown for joining music and poetry in many different forms. It probably started with what Homer did thousands of years ago on a ship, rapping out *The Iliad* and *The Odyssey*, accompanied by a musician. Then look at what Langston Hughes did in the 30's and 40's with musical friends in Harlem, but said was never done formally in public (which he told me about in detail when we collaborated in 1965 in writing a cantata, "Let Us Remember," a work for chorus, soloists and symphony orchestra performed at the San Francisco Opera House shortly before he died). After that came Mingus and Kenneth Patchen, Ferlinghetti and Stan

Getz, Jim Morrison with the Doors, Gil Scott Heron, the Last Poets ... all added their own creativity over the years, following what Jack and I started that rainy afternoon in October 1957.

What I did when playing with Dizzy Gillespie, Oscar Pettford, Mingus and Lord Buckley before and since I met Kerouac in 1956, now has reemerged, with thousands of new exciting and innovative musicians and poets, as Spoken Word.

In HipHop and Rap there is a new ever-changing series of vibrant traditions being created and re-created every day nearly 50 years after our Brata Gallery efforts, as part of our New Millennium's innovations.

Jack and I called what we did "music/poetry-poetry/music." We had already done it many times before our readings with Hart and Lamantia, always spontaneously, whenever and whereever the spirit moved us. On park benches, at each other's and friends apartments, at Bring Your Own Bottle parties at painters lofts (it was at a B.Y.O.B. party at a painter's loft where Jack and I began to do this together in 1956), at coffee houses, art openings and the jazz clubs where I performed, usually after 2 a.m. for a handful of mostly zonked out but enthusiastic New York night owls.

We never once rehearsed. We did listen intently to one another. I never drowned out one word of whatever Jack was reading or making up on the spot. When I did my spontaneous scatting (today called freestyling) he would play piano or bongos and he never drowned out or stepped on a word or interrupted a thought that I or whoever else joined us had percolating in the late night-early morning world where we were doing all this, usually for a handful of people.

We had mutual respect for one another, and anyone who joined us received the same respect. We almost never used a microphone. Most of the time, there weren't any available.

With the second coming of music/poetry-poetry/music in the Sixties, all that we did for fun in the Fifties (and those of us here always will continue to do for the joy of collaboration, whether for good pay or for free), suddenly had an audience of which we never dreamed during our spontaneous forays.

Today, I have the treat of playing with, as well as for, high school and college students, at folk festivals, jazz festivals, with poets young and old, well known actors, my own daughter Adira, people who have never read in public before, and even at symphony concerts I have conducted (at the Kennedy Center, with the National Symphony and the late E.G. Marshall reading the same parts of *On the Road* that Jack and I did before it was published. We dreamed of doing with music I would create for symphonic accompaniment, but I had to wait until 1995, 26 years after Jack's death).

In addition to playing with and for a small army of poets and musicians each year for the final day of Lowell Celebrates Kerouac, at the annual Kerouac Writer's Residence Festival in Orlando, Florida, and at a series of Insomniacathons with the indomitable Ron Whitehead in Holland, London, Louisville, New Orleans, Nashville and New York, I played for poets in Japan (including when they read in Japanese) and for readers in French, German, Portuguese, Spanish, and Italian.

In Montreal, I did the Jack Kerouac Tribute for the OFF Festival du Jazz in 2002 in Franglais (freestyling in French and English). Jack and I did this all the time.

In a memorable weekend in the Dutch town of Goes, I first played for Bob Holman when he read. He knocked me out with his spirit, his original style, his humor and his support of others. I sensed after a few minutes that he knew that we were put here to create in any way we felt in our hearts that we should, and that when you are lucky enough to be able to command the attention of others, it is your responsibility to, as Dizzy Gillespie told me when I played for his 70th birthday, "put something back into the pot."

I could see that Bob was interested in more than himself. Bob, like Ron Whitehead, wanted to turn on the World on to poetry and music, and make the very best of the arts a part of everyday life for everyone. He wanted to encourage people to be creative and observant of the beauty that surrounded us in everyday life.

Both of them were, as all of us were taught to be in our era, *inclusive*, not ex-clusive.

A few years after the first of our many performances together, Bob told me that his exciting dream of opening up a new venue for poetry and music was about to become a reality. I was invited by Bob and Danny Shot to play for the first event at the Bowery Poetry Club, in *Long Shot* magazine's tribute to Gregory Corso, even though the Club was not officially open and still under construction.

I knew that night of February 3, 2002, as we all stood with our overcoats on, drinking red wine from paper cups in the bone chilling cold, (there was still no heat) that the Bowery Poetry Club would become another milestone in New York's long history of great places to come and celebrate our artists past and present, and also celebrate one another. This was because Bob Holman was applying the principles of organic farming. He was enriching the soil for future generations by building a place that would celebrate life and creativity, rather than another rip-off sleasezoid Temple of Eurotrash for the hearing impaired, created by adults with no purpose in life except to separate kids from their money, under the guise of being CuttingEdge-Trendy-PostModern-Hip- Nihilistic-Landfill-Bound Payola Promoted Plastic Putrescence. (Fortunately, I am not judgmental, just observant.)

Bob Holman, like an increasing number of people around the world, was looking for something a little more real. He felt that we all deserve something better. Holman wanted to build a place that celebrated creativity and community through the magic of the arts, a place where anybody and everybody of any age and interest could hang out and feel part of it all.

By good fortune, all four dates were sandwiched between my other gigs across the country, where I do the work I love most to do, which pays for my kids' schooling, feeding the farm animals, groceries, taxes and everyday survival.

Still, as a year-round seven-day-a-week just-turned 72-year-old worker, I heed the advice of the late great Tompkins Square philosopher, Ukrainian Ernie, who lived close to me in 1955, only a few blocks from where the Bowery Poetry Club now stands. He gave me some advice on how to live when he found out that I played in the Charles Mingus Quintet in the fall of 1955.

Ukrainian Ernie would always help out people in the neighborhood, where I lived six flights up, at 319 E. 8th St. (before it was torn down and rebuilt in the past few years). He explained to all who would listen, how he came to America and fell in love with the New World. He always read books in English, slowly but thoroughly, about American history, poetry, novels and stories of the Old West. Ernie used to talk about how he studied the American Indian tradition of the Potlach, or Giveaway. How the most respected and revered person in the tribe was the one who was the most generous, not the greediest. And how as an immigrant, he loved the openness and spirit of this country, and how the spirit of generosity that the Potlach symbolized in this country also existed in the Old Country among the farmers in the Ukraine, where he lived as a little boy, despite how hard as it was to survive there.

"Maybe you become big shot someday. No matter. If you no can give it away, you don't got it. Indian people say if you just selfish greedy, you get all dry up and you worth nuttin'!"

Whether any of us in today's Full Greed Ahead society still "got it" is a day-by-day challenge to retain, but I know that being with a group of visionaries and sincere artists to play in a warm, affordable, inclusive, inviting environment, and being able to pay homage to all my old friends who are no longer with us, is an experience neither my friends nor my own three kids would want to miss. And if Ukrainian Ernie were still alive, he would be at the Bowery Poetry Club every night, sharing his often incredible raps with everybody.

At the Bowery Poetry Club, the words and music are a gateway to a larger communal experience. NOT a nonexistent "Movement" or secret society.

None of the places where we hung out together in the 1950s were considered Official Headquarters of the Beat Generation. None of us ever described ourselves as being part of a beat generation. It was an organization that never existed – until we were told about it years later. There were no doormen at the Cedar Bar, the Kettle of Fish, the Five Spot, the Village Gate, the Gaslight, Folk City and countless places we gathered to commune with one another. They were like the Bowery Poetry Club. These places were our meeting place for the moment. Neither Kerouac, Ginsberg, Corso, Ferlinghetti, McClure, Diane DiPrima, Neal Cassady, Charlie Parker, Monk, Gillespie, artists Joan Mitchell, Franz Kline, Pollack, DeKoonig, myself and thousands of others, ever had a secret handshake, a membership card, a letterhead, an arranged summit conference like the board of directors of the Mafia, the Elks Club, the Shriners, the 4-H Club (I belonged to that as a kid on a Pennsylvania farm in the 30's) the Trilateral Commission or The Ten Days That Shook the World.

We were all acquainted on some level with one another. We were all inspired by one another. Most of us met one another at places like The Bowery Poetry Club.

It is a blessing to have this new meeting place in New York, and hopefully it will encourage people all over the country, and through the Internet and World, to create similar places in all communities, to suit the individual needs of each place.

Since several people were surprised to see I was playing at the Bowery Poetry Club so often during this period, I thought I would write Bob Holman and the readers of *All About Jazz/New York* a note to tell him, and everyone else who wants to create their own small meeting places, why I was so happy to be there.

Musicians, poets, painters and everyday people from all walks of life are now able to determine for themselves what we would like to share with one another. We need beauty, inspiration and uplifting expression of lasting value, no matter in what form, for our artistic consumption, with as many styles and varieties as there are artists who create them. Song writers, opera singers, classical composers, rappers, folk musicians and symphony orchestras are now putting out their own CDs, and using the Internet to let people know about it.

This is happening all over the country, and is exciting. It means you can record with the idea of making the recording a document of lasting value that is the very best you can possibly do. You can find places around the country where it is possible to share what you are doing, to give you the feedback and energy to do it better.

The Bowery Poetry Club is one example that small is beautiful. All of America's cities should have venues like this on every block.

letter & lyrics

**GARY LAWLESS**

# Leon Came Back

Leon came back
all broken up inside
now he's livin' in the trailer
mama's livin' in the doublewide

he's got a bullet on a necklace
he wears it on his chest
says he can't go out without it
says he wouldn't feel dressed

there's panic at the grocery
panic in the street
he can't go out shopping now
he orders out to eat

Leon came back all broken up inside
says he knows he should have bought it
he knows he should have died
now he's livin' in the trailer
mama's livin' in the double wide

Leon bought a Harley and he
likes to take a ride
he sells a little oxy
for some money on the side

He likes to stay warm
and he likes to stay dry
he likes a snort of heroin
to help him stay high

Leon came back all broken up inside
he says he's a survivor
but he doesn't know why
he lived through all the dying
he lived through all the blood
now his life is running through him
like a wild raging flood

Leon came back from the other side
Leon came back all busted up inside
now Leon's in the trailer and
momma's in the double wide

**ROBERT YEHLING**

# Holy Child Blues

*(as performed at Cornelia St. Cafe, Greenwich Village, NY)*

**Refrain:**
You're a holy child, brave holy child
The new light of this age,
Society's crushed your hopes and dreams
You've responded with pure rage

Oh holy child, brave holy child,
Just open up your heart
To feel the awesome sacredness—
Your soul is our fresh start

**I**
They say you're a menace to society
A subject full of rage,
You barely reach the judge's chest
They're jailing you today
For making a very big mistake
How could you ever know?
Your mama's sick, your daddy's dead
You sold a little blow
To feed yourself, to clothe your sis
Your intentions all so pure
For inside that twisted angry mask
A soul shines bright and pure

**(Refrain)**

**II**
You sit inside an eight-by-ten
Your cellmate's doing life
He brags about his dirty deeds

And the way he killed his wife
It breaks your heart to hear this man
Rejoice in his violent ways
You wish you could resurrect the wife
And sweep her woes away
To redeem yourself, to give your sis
A place to live and sleep
For word's come in, she's hiding out
Word is, she's gone in deep

**(Refrain)**

**III.**
How can we relate to a society
That throws its young away?
That orders holy tender souls
To win or else you'll pay,
These precious sacred souls of love
Teardrops of angels' light,
The holy saviors of our time
And we flush them out like shit,
We flush them out like shit,
We say, you lose that's it!
You lose, you lose that's it!
I swear I do not understand
How we can face each day,
When we've killed the holy spirit
Of these kids, in every way!

**IV.**

You've helped so many inmates read,
They're gonna set you free,
A few months shy of seventeen
You've done time for you and me,
That's what they tell us on the streets,
You're a dreg of society

They had to send you up the creek
To appease their propriety
Here's twenty bucks, another chance
Do not come back again,
Oh holy child, dear holy child
I pray you find your way,
I pray you find your way,
I pray you find your way.

(From *The Voice,* a novel by Robert Yehling. ©2010 Robert Yehling.)

book excerpts

# MICHAEL BLAKE

# Excerpt from *Into the Stars*

Editor's note:

*What you might not expect to find on a World War I battlefield, you very well would expect to discover in Michael Blake's forthcoming novella—a man's enduring love for an animal, this time, a horse. Anyone who read Blake's 2009 memorial-memoir,* Twelve The King, *experienced how deep his love for a rescued wild horse was and how that love lasted long after the animal died of old age having lived on Blake's southern Arizona ranch for 15 years of its life.*

Into the Stars, *tells the tale of an American doughboy, Ledyard Dixon, stranded behind enemy lines following a fierce engagement. Dixon's miraculous survival of the battle merely sets the stage for a quixotic adventure worthy a storyteller with the Academy Award winner's imagination. Explicit, numbing description of hellish trench warfare brings to mind, but impossible, first-hand experience.*

*Blake stretches the plausible when his protagonist returns to the Allied lines with plans to not only keep the horse he found but to have it moved far beyond harm's way.*

*In addition to the powerful descriptive writing, the book is beautifully illustrated by renowned watercolorist, John Solie. Nineteen illustrations precede each chapter of the 250 page, 8 ½ x 11, hardbound book. The book may soon become available in a soft cover format without the art. Blake has also recorded the book himself for CD and/or mp3 distribution.*

*In this chapter, "In The Trees," Ledyard meets his new four-legged, battleground, travelling companion.*

\* \* \*

# In The Trees

By the time he made the edge of the woods walking consisted solely of forcing one foot to follow another. Every cell clamored for rest but finding the edge of the woods partially destroyed he willed himself deeper into the trees. The ground rose slightly upward as he staggered toward its apex. The trees were so thick that they were only inches apart in places but on reaching the top they opened into a tiny clearing. There Ledyard collapsed, falling into a deep sleep almost as he hit the ground.

When he woke his nose was filled with the wholesome fragrance of young grass. Something was climbing his earlobe and reaching back he captured a small, green beetle that he studied as it navigated the creases in his palm. He watched the beetle with a wonder he had not known since childhood. What a marvel it was in all its aspects. And what a delight to watch something whole, a creature at peace with itself and its environment.

A bird sang and, shading his eyes against the bright sunlight, he quickly found it standing on a low limb a few feet above him. The bird too filled him with a sense of awe. It fluffed its feathers, breathed through its mouth, swiveled its head, hopped from foot to foot and cocked a round, wet eye at Ledyard, singing all the time. He got the feeling that the bird was performing for him, showing all the magnificent things it could do and when it leapt into space and took flight Ledyard made light applause with his hands.

He stared up through the trees and reckoned the angle of the sun put the life of day past noon. He opened a tin of beef, washed it down with half a canteen of water, brushed the dried mud from his uniform, removed all traces of it's presence and set off to explore the woods.

The reconnaissance did not take long. The trees were not so much a woods as they were an island, roughly rectangular in shape. Though he was not good at figuring such things Ledyard estimated that he was hidden in two or three acres of trees.

On each side there was open space. One led back into no-man's land. The other faced an open meadow, maybe half a mile across which fed into the flight line of a small, enemy air base.

Beyond the wide meadow was another line of trees but there was no way to tell how deep they might be. He would have to cross to them at nightfall and Ledyard sat at the edge of the trees, smoking cigarettes as he watched what little activity there was at the sleepy airfield. During the time he watched, which was much of the afternoon, only one plane swooped down the length of the long meadow and landed.

It was late afternoon before he started back, his plan being to sleep awhile before crossing the meadow in the middle of night. As he walked up the incline it occurred to him that it would be a nice idea to sit out the war in this little wood. His mind jumped a step further, entertaining the thought that it wouldn't be bad to spend the rest of his life here. He hadn't been in the war very long but it had been enough to sour him on the whole human race. Individuals were one thing, people like Drayton Witt, but the race itself, when left to its own devices...a tremor of loathing ran up his spine.

Humankind was a wash. This never-ending war had been deadlocked for years, long before the Americans jumped into it. There were no winners when it came to a conflict like the Great War. The biggest dolt to ever wear a uniform could see that. The best an individual could hope for was to somehow survive it.

The best the world could hope for was that it would somehow burn itself out someday. Humankind had distinguished itself in but two ways Ledyard thought. It had demonstrated a tremendous capacity for incompetence and an insatiable appetite for carnage.

'Ledyard, the beetles and the birds,' he thought, chuckling to himself.

'That beats anything going on outside these trees.'

His idyll was broken by the sounds of bright, happy voices, German voices, filtering down to him from the high point in the wood. Freezing, Ledyard listened, trying to get a fix on them. After a few seconds he could tell that the voices were stationary.

He glanced about him. There was silence from everywhere but above. He crept forward on all fours, taking great care to make no sound with his hands or knees. A few minutes of crawling brought him close enough to see the heads of men, pilots from the airfield he guessed. They were the picture of confident, Germanic youth, and they were picnicking in the very spot he had made his bed the night before.

He contemplated tossing one of his grenades into their midst but the more he thought about it the less it appealed to him. What could he possibly gain from doing something like that? Practically, it would be nothing but a blazing, noisy advertisement for himself, only hastening his own death. And what would blowing up a group of picnicking pilots actually accomplish? Would it shorten the war? He thought not.

A strange thought popped into his head. Who won didn't matter nearly so much as putting an end to wholesale destruction. That would be the greatest victory of all. And the only one.

Keeping his eyes on the pilots, Ledyard backtracked down the slope. When he was out of their view he got to his feet and tramped to the far end of the wood, looking for a spot where he could conceal himself. He found a deadfall not far from the meadow and after thirty minutes of digging out a hollow he had constructed a safe, dry chamber. He wedged himself in, covering the opening as thoroughly as possible. Folding his arms in front of his chest, he shut his eyes and began to rehearse the nocturnal trek he would make when the moon was up and the war was asleep.

His own sleep was so deep and so luxurious that he barely stirred. When he finally opened his eyes again it was daylight. Ledyard groaned with dismay as he pushed away the branches that covered his hiding place.

He sat on the log that had sheltered him and fished out the remaining pieces of gray meat floating in his last tin of beef. Then he drank the grease and swallowed what was left of his water.

'Well, now I'm in for it,' he thought, pushing an errant drop of water from his lip back into his mouth.

It was early morning and he would have to go thirsty and hungry all day before making his getaway. In the meantime he would check the clearing at the top of the hill for scraps left behind by the picnickers.

Lifting himself off the log, he thought of the meadow again and gazed in that direction with the idea of re-estimating its width and the time it would take to get across.

A riderless horse was standing just beyond the tree line, its neck arching over the earth as it nibbled the most promising shoots of grass. It wore no saddle but a bridle was intact about its head, the reins trailing lazily behind as the horse browsed.

Ledyard moved to the edge of the trees and the horse jerked its head up and stared at him.

"Hello there," Ledyard said softly, raising his hand in a gesture of peace.

The horse stared a moment longer then returned to its browsing. Ledyard took a step forward and the animal moved a step in the opposite direction.

'Typical,' Ledyard thought. If there was one thing he knew about horses it was that they loved playing hard to get. Many animals used that behavior as an everyday form of revenge on the human race but horses were the masters.

He watched the animal a few moments longer, gauging the sincerity of his aloofness. The horse was watching him too and Ledyard decided that his commitment was flimsy.

"Okay," he called softly, "I'll see you then."

He walked the few steps back to the deadfall. On the way he glanced over his shoulder. The horse's head was up, watching him go.

Ledyard rolled under the log and waited. It wasn't long before he heard the first tentative footfalls of the big animal as it moved into the trees. Not wanting to startle him, Ledyard began to hum a little tune. The plop of his footsteps came closer and closer, then stopped. Ledyard twisted slowly out from his hiding place and looked up, straight into the curious face hanging over him. The horse was peering down from the other side of the log.

"Hi," Ledyard said, getting to his feet.

He stretched out a hand and let the horse sniff his fingers. Then he sat down submissively on the log and began to stroke his soft muzzle, gently taking up one of the free hanging reins in the process.

The horse was perfectly amenable to being captured and stood still as Ledyard made a tour of his body, running hands over the neck, withers, back, rump, legs and belly. The horse carried no wounds and had good muscle. He'd been shod recently and his short, dark coat glistened with good health. Whoever had been in charge of him had kept him in excellent shape.

"You one of ours, or one of theirs?" Ledyard asked when he reached his head again.

The horse looked at him quizzically.

"Too smart to answer, eh?"

The horse sighed deeply and gazed off through the trees as if he couldn't be bothered with such trivialities. Laughing at his new companion's disdain, Ledyard laid a hand on his neck and said…

"Well, let's take a walk."

He stepped forward and the horse, with an ease that might have indicated years of togetherness, stepped right along with him.

They revisited the scene of the pilot's picnic but found nothing but a flock of yellow-eyed blackbirds. The grass was good and Ledyard let the horse browse until he lost interest. Then they made a round of inspections.

The no-man's land from which Ledyard had emerged was still a graveyard and the airfield was sleepy as ever.

Ledyard wanted to distance himself from the enemy and they tramped the length of the trees, stopping at the end furthest from the airfield, there to wait for night.

By mid-afternoon the horse was becoming impatient with waiting and Ledyard, knowing he was getting thirsty, tried to keep him moving.

His own thirst had become profound. He had even put a pebble under his tongue to stimulate saliva and keep his mouth moist but hours had passed and a little wetness on his tongue was no longer enough. He was having trouble thinking about anything but water.

The tension was building in both of them and, though it was still two hours before sunset, Ledyard decided he would get onto the horse's back. At the least it would break the monotony of waiting. And it would tell him something about who was going to carry him across half a mile of meadow after dark.

Taking the reins in one hand, he patted the horse's back to let him know what was coming and swung up. The transformation in his compliant companion was instantaneous and remarkable.

The horse tucked his chin toward his chest and began to dance slowly in place, every muscle at the ready. He was coiling for action but at the same time was not at all unmanageable. Ledyard cued him with light pressure from one heel and they moved off through the trees. His walk was more like a glide, free and airy yet beautifully controlled. His mouth was extraordinarily light, the slightest tug on the reins inducing him to halt. After a few steps Ledyard knew that he was sitting astride an animal that was superior in every way.

The clank and grind of heavy equipment was droning in the distance. They halted and listened. A few more steps brought them within view of the battlefield, a view that revealed a terrible spectacle.

Dozens of tanks, escorted by hundreds of ground troops were headed their way. To one man on a horse it looked like half the German army was coming.

Wheeling about, they hurried back the way they had come. When they reached the apron of the meadow again Ledyard tried to think of suitable options but nothing was available. There would be no way to conceal himself from what was coming and what was coming would be here long before dark.

With a cluck to the horse they moved onto the meadow at a calculated walk. If they were seen by anyone at the airfield a walk was more likely to arouse curiosity than suspicion.

They had traveled barely fifty yards when Ledyard heard an engine start up and seconds later a bi-plane was lifting shakily into the air. Ledyard cursed his luck. Not only had someone decided to put a plane up at the same time he was crossing but the wind had conspired against him as well. It was coming his way.

The fragile plane, bobbing like a cork in the air, would pass directly overhead in a few seconds. Ledyard glanced at the trees in the distance. There was no way he could make it without being seen and it was too late to go back. He walked on, watching the approach of the plane from the corner of his eye.

Its nose dropped and it swerved toward him to get a look at the man on the horse.

Ledyard could no longer ignore the oncoming plane. Pulling up he stood and waited as the aircraft sunk lower and lower, its blurred propeller aimed directly at him.

He had planned to wave but as the plane zoomed in he sensed a lethal intent. His arm had just gone into the air when he made a last second decision to bolt. Spinning around, they shot toward the trees from whence they had come, Ledyard laying low on the horse's neck.

His sixth sense saved both their lives. Just as they dug for the trees the plane's machine gun opened up, spraying deadly fire over the spot they had occupied.

The horse's speed was tremendous and they regained the trees in what seemed like no time. Holding him with one hand Ledyard placed the other on his rump and twisted his head for a look back. The plane had already climbed high into the sky and was executing a long, lazy turn. It was coming back.

As he watched it drop back down to skim the surface of the meadow Ledyard felt certain that it was not going to bother hunting for him in the trees. It was going to land and report the sighting.

Reaching over his shoulder, he pulled one of the grenades out of the pack on his back. Grabbing up a hunk of the horse's mane he waited until what he thought was the opportune moment and digging his heels into the horse's flanks, burst back into the open at a full run. His hope was to try to intersect the plane at a right angle, thereby avoiding the machine gun.

The plane lurched awkwardly in his direction but was too late to meet him dead on. As they came together he could see the goggled faces of two men staring at him from the cockpit.

Ledyard sat straight up on the running horse, pulled the pin with his teeth and heaved the bomb as high and far into the air as he could.

The grenade exploded in mid-air, near one of the wing tips. It did not hit the plane and for a moment Ledyard thought he had failed. But either the concussion or the surprise of his attack caused one of the wings to dip crazily toward the earth. As the aircraft's wing dropped lower and lower Ledyard pulled up to watch.

By the time it reached the vicinity of the air field it was flying practically perpendicular to the ground and Ledyard knew it was going to crash. Suddenly, it cartwheeled onto its nose, bounced into the air and came to ground with a faint, reverberating thud.

Ledyard and the horse galloped for the tree line and when they made the woods he pulled up and looked down the meadow for the last time. There were flames and a column of black smoke, billowing into the sky above the airfield.

*To follow the book's publication progress, visit* http://www. hrymfaxe.com/index.html

**KELLY THACKER**

Editor's note:

*Before turning to the chapter from William Thompson Ong's forthcoming historical novel,* The Lake *set in Johnstown, Pennsylvania in 1889, we invite you to read a perfect introduction: "What If?" by Kelly Thacker. Her essay explores what might have happen in the aftermath of the Johnstown Flood if the world had been as litigious then as it is today.*

\* \* \*

# What If?

On May 31, 1889, after several days of relentless rainfall, the poorly constructed dam in South Fork, Pennsylvania burst, sending twenty million tons of water raging down a mountain to Johnstown, Pennsylvania. The death toll was over two thousand people, killing entire families and nearly wiping out the entire town. Nearly every family lost at least one member; no one was immune to loss. The Johnstown flood is known as one of the worst disasters in our nation's history.

The dam belonged to the South Fork Fishing and Hunting Club, owned by Andrew Carnegie, Henry Clay Frick and Andrew Mellon, among others. The owners of the club refused to believe the dam was unsafe and inadequately maintained, despite concerns raised by the Cambria Ironworks downstream. These owners also ravaged the nearby countryside, stripping it of the surrounding lumber which would afford protection when Mother Nature decided to send her unprecedented downpour. Very few repairs were actually rendered to the dam. Of those few, a miserly amount was spent, without any accompanying engineering knowledge. Leaks were repaired with mud and straw. Discharge pipes at the base of the dam had been removed the previous year. The club owners were wealthy and exclusive; the people of Johnstown were poor industrial workers, resulting in little thought being given to these working class people downstream.

There are two great books on the subject, *In Sunlight, In a Beautiful Garden,* a novel by Kathleen Cambor and *The Johnstown Flood,* by David McCullough. McCullough, particularly, has put together a stark and powerful story of the history behind the disaster and the outcome of the flood. When the ensuing lawsuits were brought against these wealthy owners of this dam that wreaked such devastation and loss of life, the outcome was zilch, zippo, nada. The Carnegies and Mellons had immense wealth and enormous power. Even the newspapers, while railing against the owners of the dam, never mentioned names.

Imagine standing at the second story window of your house, the rising water having already consumed the first floor and its contents, listening to the ear-shattering roar, watching your screaming friends and neighbors being sucked from their homes as the force of the water stripping the clothes from their backs. They are accompanied by uprooted trees, houses, furniture, and dead livestock. Think of fighting for your life in the racing, frigid water, hearing the cries of your children above the roar and being powerless to save them while you fight to escape a thirty-ton railroad car bearing down upon you. Picture the devastation in the hideously, dead quiet of the morning after, staring out across town at mud, rock, planks, shingles, houses crushed and broken or lying belly up, dead animals, human corpses and unthinkable destruction, being unable to decipher where your house used to be with no landmark to guide you. And if you were lucky enough to survive, then standing above your own needs of dealing with the loss of all your worldly possessions was the more critical priority of finding your lost loved ones and praying they had somehow miraculously survived – then tending to the staggering amount of injured, and finding drinking water and food. It is difficult to imagine the sheer hopelessness.

One of the reasons the Johnstown flood fascinates me is because I own a court reporting firm. We live in a litigious society. If there's even a whiff of a possible lawsuit in the air, an attorney will sniff it out. Lawsuits of every shape, size and color abound, bordering on the ridiculous. In fact, on any given day, you can Google class action lawsuits and join myriad litigations: Your credit card company overcharged you; your cell phone is sickening you with harmful cancer rays; you may have stubbed your toe at Wal-Mart.

America has gone overboard when it comes to litigation. After thirty-plus years in the business, I've seen enough unnecessary lawsuits to last several lifetimes.

But in my expert opinion, this catastrophic event merited the lawsuits that followed. When I dwell too long on it, I feel anger and outrage at the injustice and unfairness of those elite and wealthy men walking away scot-free. How could the citizens of an entire town lose everything without some form of remuneration, however small in measure?

*But, what if?*

McCullough writes, "In the judgment of lawyers who have examined the facts of the disaster in recent years, it seems likely that had the damage cases been conducted according to today's standards, the club and several of its members would have lost. It is even conceivable that some of those immense Pittsburgh fortunes would have been reduced to almost nothing." McCullough goes on to say it may have even altered the nation's industrial growth.

This is an extremely sobering thought.

*What if* Andrew Carnegie had lost his vast wealth as a result of these lawsuits? He made his fortune in the steel industry, forming the Keystone Bridge Company in 1862 and converting rickety wooden railroad bridges into steel. He went on to form the Carnegie Steel Company and later U.S. Steel. In 1889, the year of the flood, the Carnegie Steel Company made a profit of $40 million ($900 million in today's dollars). At the end of his life, Carnegie became a philanthropist, giving away $350 million – worth $9 billion today – and using a portion of that money to build over three thousand libraries.

*If* Carnegie had not been responsible for converting the untold number of unsafe wooden trestle bridges into steel, how many lives would have been lost due to railroad accidents? If you traced the lost lives to future generations, how many people would not be alive today?

And what about Pittsburgh and its rich heritage in the steel business? Where would the history of our nation be without the literary and cultural history sequestered in three thousand libraries?

Carnegie's partner in the steel business was Henry Clay Frick. Frick was famous for supplying the coke needed to make steel. *If* he had lost his fortune in these lawsuits, what would the history of coke in the steel industry be? With his vast fortune, he erected six buildings in downtown Pittsburgh. What would the history of the city be without these buildings?

Of the many things Andrew Mellon is known for, financing aluminum and coke is at the forefront. He created an entire industry of turning industrial waste into coal-gas, coal-tar and sulfur. He financed Charles Martin Hall's discovery of smelting aluminum, still the only process used to make aluminum worldwide. *If* Mellon had lost his fortune in the Johnstown flood lawsuits, how could the world possibly absorb the loss of his contribution to the industrial revolution?

*If* Carnegie and Mellon had lost their fortunes, where would the world be without the Carnegie Mellon University?

Carnegie, Mellon, Frick. Three major players in the deaths caused by the Johnstown flood, and three major players in the U.S. industrial revolution and the city of Pittsburgh. *If* these three men had been forced to pay damages in the lawsuits, how would it have altered the American industrial revolution? Would Pittsburgh be the city it is today?

It's an interesting conundrum: Justice being served with restitution to the grieving loved ones of over 2,000 dead versus the non-existence of these men's contribution to the industrial revolution. *If* these family members had received large settlements, blue collar workers may have become white collar workers. Scores of children may have received college educations, resulting in the ability to take far different paths in their lives. *History may have been altered.*

*If* these men's contributions to the industrial revolution had not taken place, the railroad, aluminum and steel industries might not be the same as they are today. *History may have been altered.*

**WILLIAM THOMPSON ONG**

Editor's note:

*In this chapter from William Thompson Ong's historical novel,*
The Lake, *protagonist Caleb McBride, an Irish schoolteacher
incensed by the threat posed by a dam high above blue-collar
Johnstown in central Pennsylvania, confronts wealthy Pittsburgh
socialite Angus Prescott with the "smoking gun"—an engineering
report revealing the dam's defects. Caleb is hopelessly in love with
Angus's beautiful, renegade daughter, Annabelle, who witnesses the
uninvited guest's humiliation.*

# The Uninvited Guest

The moment his eyes opened late the next morning, Caleb knew
what his mission was. He threw on his suit and slipped into his
walking shoes. He stuffed the *Morrell Report* inside a satchel. Dora
made him an omelet, and by noon he was on his way to the railroad
station.

He bought a round trip ticket for Pittsburgh. Once aboard, he
studied the map Annabelle had drawn in one of her letters. He
arrived at the station in the early evening. Once outside, he glanced
at the directions for the bridge to Allegheny City and began walking.

One hour later, he arrived at a sign for Ridge Avenue. Turning
right as the map indicated, he arrived ten minutes later at a pair of
menacing wrought iron gates. In the fading light he could make out
the name *Prescott* on the gatepost.

Caleb slipped through the shrubbery and walked past more than
a dozen landaus parked in the circular drive, their polished black
cabs gleaming in torchlight that cast shadows on a mansion the size
of an English castle.

The coachmen were lounging and chatting among themselves.
Caleb had no idea what they were doing there, nor did he care. He
was on a life-or-death mission to find one man—the man who could
do something about the dam. Nothing was going to stand in his way.

The front door was partially open. Within seconds, he was inside.

A man in a butler's uniform came striding up. "Excuse me, sir," he said. "May I help you?" The man's alarmed stare clashed with Caleb's stare of utter determination.

"I must speak with Angus Prescott. It's a matter of extreme urgency."

The man's eyes narrowed. "I am afraid that will not be possible tonight. Mr. Prescott is quite busy at the moment."

"I am not leaving until I see him."

"Impossible, sir."

Caleb's eyes roamed the foyer. To the right he saw a long hallway, at the far end of which was a door slightly ajar. He heard the sound of laughter and started toward it. The butler moved in front of him.

Being a foot taller and more agile, Caleb pushed him aside and scurried down the hallway, the butler following, shouting for him to stop.

• • •

They all seemed to hear the commotion at the same moment, turning and looking toward the door of the magnificent room glowing with candled chandeliers and bedecked in flower arrangements that would have drawn admiring glances at Buckingham Palace.

Everyone was there. The Whitneys had joined the Astors and Vanderbilts, coming down by train from New York in the Carnegie's private car, to merge with the Pittsburgh contingent, which included the Fricks, Pitcairns, Phipps, and Mellons.

Angus sat at the head of the table. At the other end was Harriet and on either side of her, Annabelle and Francis Bellamy.

When Caleb McBride banged through the doorway bearing the grim warning of the *Morrell Report*, he couldn't stop himself. It took only the length of a single nine-word sentence for his mind to register that he had charged into the lion's den. His voice responded by sliding downhill from bold pronouncement to apologetic whimper.

"Mr. Prescott, you must do something about the dam."

What happened next was like the long moment of embarrassed silence at the end of a dreadful theatrical performance. Caleb stood like a mummy, his body frozen in panic.

Between Angus and Harriet stood a dozen men in black penguin suits and shirts boiled stiff with starch, their women partners in gorgeous silk dresses and hats—dear God in Heaven, the hats! These concoctions of feathery plumes were ripped from half the waterfowl of Florida—white herons, spoonbills, and snowy egrets rising and falling, nodding and swaying every time a feminine head made the slightest move. It was the jury from Aviary Hell.

*Annabelle!*—thank God she was there! Caleb saw her lips begin to move. Yes, it would be his dear, beloved Annabelle who would be the first to break the silence, throw him a rope and pull him to safety.

"Caleb!"—she shrieked it at the top of her lungs.

This was followed by Harriet's slow sigh as the words oozed from pursed lips.

"May God in Heaven save us all!"

The room fell silent. Angus rose and began walking toward Caleb. Along his way Andrew Carnegie thrust out a hand and grabbed him by the sleeve.

"What have we here, Angus?" Carnegie grinned. "Someone late for dinner?"

Angus stood facing Caleb, who reached into the satchel and pulled out the yellowing bulk of pages. Angus grabbed the document, flipped through it, and handed it back.

"Calm down, Mr. McBride. This is hardly the time or the place . . . Perhaps I could arrange for you to address the Board . . . ."

Carnegie waved his hand and tapped his wine glass with a spoon. "Over half the board is in the room at this very moment. And you, Angus, make it a quorum."

Nobody else at the table seemed especially happy with the suggestion. Eyebrows had already risen, but now voices began whispering.

"What are you waiting for, Angus?" Carnegie's grin grew bigger. "Call the meeting to order."

But it was Harriet's steely voice that came down like a hammer. "He will do no such thing, Andrew."

Angus gripped Caleb's arm. He turned him around and steered him toward the door where the butler stood surrounded by a handful of waiters with sleeves rolled up.

"I am afraid you must leave, young man. But you will have your meeting, I promise you that."

Looking over his shoulder, Caleb saw Annabelle staring back at him—along with everyone else. From her expression, he couldn't tell what she was thinking. Feeling Angus's hand mercifully guiding him to freedom was enough to prompt a final apology.

"Thank you, sir. . . I am truly sorry . . . I did not mean to interrupt . . . but thank you for the meeting."

Caleb went through the door, and the butler closed it after him. The table began buzzing with shocked chatter.

"I am so embarrassed," Harriet said for everyone to hear.

"Embarrassed?" Carnegie asked. "I thought the young man showed some real gumption." He turned to Angus. "You should hire him to run your mill."

Annabelle rose from her chair and hurried to the door. But when she opened it and peered down the long corridor, there was no sign of Caleb. She moved down the hallway to the front door and looked out.

Caleb was nowhere to be seen.

• • •

Susan took him horseback riding to try and clear his mind.

Caleb had told her how, after the incident at the Prescott's, he had found his way to the Merriman Estate and stayed overnight with Josh. He returned on the first train in the morning.

They rode on the path along the river towards Woodvale, stopping now and then to admire the scenery.

"It's beautiful, isn't it?" Susan said.

"Yes—and the air up here is so much cleaner than Johnstown."

"Maybe it will help put things a little more into perspective."

Caleb looked at her. "I hope I didn't jeopardize my future with Annabelle."

"An embarrassing moment should not be the end of the world," Susan said.

"They were staring at me as if I were a monkey at the zoo," Caleb said. "They certainly know how to humiliate an outsider."

They rode across the river to another view just as spectacular. "At least you got yourself a meeting with the Board," Susan said.

"You sound like my father," Caleb replied. "'There's no such thing as bad weather,' he always said. 'Only different kinds of good weather.'"

Susan smiled. "When do you see Annabelle again?"

"I have no idea. Josh says she's preparing for her trip to Paris with Harriet."

"You shouldn't let how she feels stop you. When you believe in a cause as important as the dam, nothing should stand in your way."

Susan turned her horse around, and they began the ride back to Golden Gables. Caleb could feel his spirits rising. *Thank God for Susan.* She was more than a mother. She had a knack for being there exactly when he needed her—with a shoulder that, although feminine, was firm enough in wisdom for a man to lean on.

She turned to wink at Caleb. "Besides, you should be grateful. It's not every day a man gets a chance to make a fool of himself in front of the most powerful men in America."

He thought about it for a moment and nodded. Once again Susan was right. Those *were* the most powerful men in America. He would soon be facing them with a chance to convince them to take action.

Perhaps it *was* true. There was no such thing as bad weather.

• • •

When Caleb came down to dinner, Miss Ramsey was discussing the headline in the *Tribune* about Congress amending the Chinese Exclusion Act of 1882 by forbidding Chinese laborers who had left the country from returning, even with valid immigration visas. "If I had written the original act, I would have sent all the Hungarians, the Italians, the Jews, and the Negroes back to where they came from," she said. "Along with the Chinese."

"You mean deport them?" Charlie asked.

"Yes, deport every last one of them." The aging librarian removed her glasses and thought for a moment. "It would be a Diaspora in reverse. And I would even include the Irish."

"The Irish?" Pete asked, his eyes shifting along with those of all the other roomers to Caleb. "Including Mr. McBride?"

"Every last one."

"But who would work in the coal mines and steel mills to keep the nation's commerce humming?" Charlie asked. "Who would do the dirty work so that people like Andrew Carnegie can make his millions and we can have our little luxuries?"

Caleb watched as Miss Ramsey's lips curled into a smile. "I am sure we have plenty of our own people for that," she said. "We can even raise their wages because they work twice as hard as the foreigners."

In the long silence that followed, Caleb did the only two things he could think of under the circumstances. He poured Miss Ramsey another glass of wine.

Then he flashed his big Irish smile.

ISAAC LOMELI

# Excerpt From *Tales From The Eastside*: *The Stories That Never Get Told*

All the streets are long and wide and end at the wall that separates us from the other side. You have to be home before the streetlights come on—that's the rule out here—but half the time they stay off. These streets are dark, and mine is darker than most.

This is my story, so to me it's darker, yet dearer. This is the Eastside…the other side of the tracks…the place *some* drive by, not stop by.

I've grown up here. It wasn't always this way. It used to be a decent neighborhood. I used to play in these streets. Now, I stay away from these streets. It's the eastside, so you know we got eastside problems: gangs, drugs, *Mexicans*, a liquor store, a park with more violence than play and more crying than laughing, and no pleasure without pain. People don't walk these streets, they lurk…yup, lurk. I'm not in a gang—don't want to be—and I don't do drugs; but I am Mexican—whether I like it or not. It seems I'm always on the receiving end of violence. I guess it doesn't pay to be Mr. Nice Guy in my barrio.

Speaking of violence, let me tell you about how I got here—on the Eastside.

It was the 70's and I was five. Like most Mexicans in those days, you went where there were jobs. The city was a good place to find them. I grew up on a ranch with my grandparents—my mother was a child herself when she had me, so she took some time off from mothering until she was old enough to be a mother. My grampa worked on this ranch from morning to evening, while my grama worked in the town in which we lived, taking care of old folks. Well, my mom finally decided she wanted to be a mother and take my new baby brother and me to the Valley where my new dad lived—I never did call my brother's dad "Dad." He was just Fred to me.

One night we were living some place, and Fred came home covered in blood. The next thing I knew we were in Anaheim, Calif., home of Disneyland, the happiest place on Earth.

It was a new city. The apartments we moved into were fairly new. I had never seen new buildings before, with new paint and new carpet, and new streets and sidewalks, and new trees. It sure was beautiful. Everything is beautiful when it's new.

## Disneyland

I know, I know. What an amazing place to live, down the street from Disneyland. For as long as I can remember, I knew who Mickey Mouse was. I knew all about the Mickey Mouse Club— about Goofy, and Mini, Donald, and Pluto. I would sit in front of the TV at my grandma's ranch and sing like every other American kid, M-I-C-K-E-Y-M-O-U-S-E. And, it brought joy to my young heart.

Like every other kid, it was my dream to one day go to Disneyland and shake hands with Mickey Mouse. I would never have thought that I would be living a stone's throw away…and I would have never thought it would bring me so much pain, fear, and sadness.

In this moment, life looked like a fairytale. On one side of me was Disneyland and on the other, The Big A—home of the California Angels. I was sandwiched between two dreams like peanut butter and jelly. I was a little boy who felt like everything was possible.

At one point in my life, baseball was my favorite sport, back when everyone played it *for the love of the game.* Imagine being squeezed between two of your wildest dreams. It was a dream it would soon become a reminder of everything that was just out of my reach.

Baseball aside—until another time. It was probably our first night in our new apartment. We were all quietly asleep well before 9:30 p.m. We were all nestled in bed with thoughts of Disneyland in our head. Our pictures newly hung on the wall of our new apartment, not a creature was stirring…not even Mickey Mouse.

All of a sudden, a boom and a bang. My parents, like plastic army men on their stomachs, low-crawled to the living room windows.

"GET BACK!!! Stay in your room," they shouted.

My little brother and I squeezed each other tight. The sounds grew louder and stronger. I was the oldest, so I shielded him with my body and did my best to be brave in front of him. It sounded like bombs exploding in our courtyard.  We lay there afraid, waiting for momma and daddy to tell us all was okay.

All we heard were more explosions.

Finally, after what seemed like an eternity, our parents began to scream.

"Kids…Jose, Shorty…come look."

We looked at each other and were too scared to move.

"Come! Look!" My parents screamed again.

We were frozen with fear.  Then we heard, "Hurry…you're gonna miss it."

For whatever reason, the words *you're gonna miss it* got us up out of bed and running out the door. I guess kids don't like to miss a thing.  As we approached the front door, I could see the other neighbors looking up.

What an amazing sight.  Big, bright colorful lights filled the sky. I didn't know what I was looking at until my mother said, "Come, look at the fireworks." Wow, so this was fireworks.  It was the most amazing thing my young eyes had seen.

For the first several years, fireworks were the greatest thing in my life.  I never missed them, and I always begged my mom to let us stay up until the fireworks came on.  But, eventually, this fascination lost its shine.

Today, when others look at the sky to enjoy the Fourth of July, I merely glance occasionally, and focus more on the people looking at the fireworks.  It's a reminder of wonder and amazement.  If you ever want to see what it looks like, just look at all those faces, young and old, watching those fireworks light the sky fantastic.

## E-Tickets

You always knew it was summer again.  Back in that day, fireworks season only lasted from Cinco de Mayo until Labor Day. Fireworks meant summer was on its way.

Disneyland was a treat. Even though we lived less than a mile away, our pocketbooks kept us miles apart. What a treat it was when Leroy's mother took us all to Disneyland for his birthday.  It was the greatest birthday ever. Your mother takes you and your best friends to Disneyland for your birthday? What possibly could be done to out-do that party?

It was Raymond, my brother Max, and myself. We woke up that morning with so much energy it literally felt like my insides were going to explode. There was this rush that I had never felt before. I remember being so full of joy and anxiety. I couldn't wait to see it all with my very own eyes.

This wasn't the first time I had been, but it was the first time I was going with friends. It was the first time we were going with our own game plan. It was the first time where we were in control of what we did and didn't do, what we ate and didn't eat, and roamed where we wanted to roam. It was a beautiful thing.

It started off the happiest place on earth. Until it was time to go on the big rides. That is when my joy turned to fear. The ride was Space Mountain. I had never been big enough to get on the ride before, but now I was. It was time to meet my demon. All my fears came to this crossroads. Would I take it on with bravery and honor? Or would I cower and cry away?

I'd like to tell a story of bravery and courage, that I stood tall with honor and dignity. However, I was so terrified of going on Space Mountain that when we all read the sign warning us that if we had any heart condition we should not ride, I quickly pleaded, "I've got heartburn." My young mind thought heartburn was a heart condition. I tried looking at my little brother in hopes he would save me by asking me to wait with him, but that request didn't come.

Thirty minutes of horror followed. But, like all fears, I faced it and survived it. Nonetheless, I was still afraid. It was great that I had faced my fears and lived to tell about it. But, unfortunately, I still had about three E-tickets remaining. There was a part of me that wanted to lose these tickets "accidentally," thus avoiding having to go on any more roller coasters.

What I learned from that one day is that real joy and happiness do exist, and that we cannot have either without knowing real fear and pain and loss. I learned it is better to challenge your fears than to live in them; things are always better when you share them with those closest to you. Most of all, I learned that in life we only have but a few chances to take certain rides. Use them, don't lose them.

# Courtyards

Apartments are strange in themselves. They all look the same—inside and out. They all have a courtyard and the same number of units. Our courtyard had a set of apartments facing each other that were identical—they were numbered 1-7—and I lived in lucky number seven. We lived upstairs and next to some Guedos—back when there were Guedos in the neighborhood. The barrio was still a "neighborhood". Not even half of it was Mexican.

I met my first friend in the courtyard, behind the alley from mine. He was a Guedo named Dwayne. On the other side of my courtyard was another Chinito named Kenny. And, across the street from me was the only Negrito in the neighborhood, Leroy.

A courtyard is one of the greatest things God ever invented. Our courtyard became everything from a park, to a soccer field, boxing ring, kickball field, picnic area, reception hall, and place to witness life at its best and worst. It was the hub of social life in the 'hood. Everything I needed to know, I found out in my courtyard.

In my courtyard, I learned to play hide 'n seek, freeze tag, Cowboys 'n Indians. I learned to kiss a girl. I learned that bees sting, and wasps sting twice as hard. I learned that Mexicans like to drink Budweiser and sing *corridos* at midnight.

I also learned that sap is sticky, and it hurts if you fall from a tree. I learned that I can't fly, even if I put a towel around my neck and call it a cape—like Superman. I learned that sometimes you gotta stand up and fight for what you believe is right; and sometimes, *it's best to run away and live to fight another day.* I learned how to make a fort, and I learned that a window breaks when you throw a ball at it. I learned how to chase girls, and I learned that it hurts to get kicked in the *privates.*

I learned to stand. I learned to fall. I learned to cry, and I learned to feel pain. I learned to be brave, and I learned to be afraid. I learned to have friends, and I learned to lose them. I learned the thrill of winning, and I learned to lose and the agonizing feeling that came with it. I learned to laugh, and I learned to be teased. I learned to dust myself off, and I learned shame. I learned to tattletale, and I learned to take the blame.

winter / spring 2011

Courtyards have rules. You don't just walk through anyone's courtyard and start running things and telling kids how to play tag, or kickball, or whatever game is being played. I'm *serious*…you'll get some rocks thrown your way. And, if you happen to be the kid who lives where the swimming pool is, or where the manager lives, you just have to find yourself a courtyard and earn a place there.

It is rare to have cross-courtyard mingling before the age of 10. Unless you create some sort of truce with the other courtyard, it usually doesn't happen. And, if you ever get invited to play in another courtyard, make sure you know who's in charge and give the customary greeting: "Hello, I'm just here visiting, feel free to abuse me and use me in any way you see fit, and excuse me now if I do anything to offend your way of life." This statement is never said, but implied in your eyes when you shake hands.

I'll never forget this one time when I was in the 3$^{rd}$ grade…poor David. Yup, David was a white boy. As the only white boy on the street, he lived the finer side of life when it came to toys. Well, David decided to play with us one day in Leroy's courtyard. He brought his toys—and they were nice, let me tell you. Raymond, the kid in charge of our courtyard came out and decided he wanted to play, too. David didn't know anything about the customary greeting. So, when Raymond came over and took David's truck to play, it got a little ugly.

"Hey, that's *my* truck," David said.

"So, I'm playing with it." Raymond gave David the opportunity to relinquish the truck without any incident.

Poor David didn't know any better. "No, it's *mine*."

The next sound we heard was the thud of the truck against David's head. Immediately following that thud were David's cries and "Momma!"

"Take your truck."

I guess Raymond was being nice that day. At least David got his truck back.

prose

## GAIL BORNFIELD

# Lunch at Annabelle's

I was sitting at a table alone in my favorite restaurant in Ketchikan having an early lunch while preparing for a busy afternoon. The waitress brought a menu for me and I glanced at it quickly. I was familiar with the offerings. She took my order for salmon chowder while setting down coffee and cream.

I stared out the window, a million thoughts running through my head. The sound of voices attracted my attention. I glanced to the door. The waitress was seating a man in his early thirties, dressed in typical Alaskan garb – jeans, t-shirt, and a flannel shirt for warmth. As he sat down, he took out a pack of cigarettes and moved it nervously through his hands. I could see his life had not been easy – lots of alcohol and drugs. His clothes were too big – perhaps not intentionally. Premature lines crossed his face. When the waitress came to the table, he ordered a double vodka on the rocks.

A woman appeared in the doorway casting a big smile in his direction. She appeared to be wearing his sweats and shirt. Perhaps she had just gotten up. He welcomed her with a broad grin and a quick kiss.

"Have you ordered?" she asked.

"Yes, just now."

She hurried off.

The waitress delivered his drink. He didn't touch it. It just sat in front of him. He lit a cigarette, taking long slow drags. He watched the door, waiting for her. He never touched the drink.

The waitress returned with two waters. He walked to the bar and asked for lemon. Returning to the table, he squeezed it into the vodka. The woman reappeared in a short blue dress with sparkles across the bodice. Even with cute curly blond hair, she appeared older than she likely was. Her face had aged way beyond her years. He smiled as he saw her.

He stood up to let her into the booth; she scooted to the inner seat. He pushed the vodka in front of her. She moved it quickly to her mouth, closing her eyes as it reached her lips. As she lowered the glass, she flashed him a look of gratitude.

The French fries arrived. He gently pushed the plate in front of her, encouraging her to eat. She pushed them away. He teased her, holding up the fries, pretending to feed her. She ate a few and reached for the vodka. He moved the water in front of her instead. She ate a few more fries, followed by a swallow of water. Smiling at him, she reached for the vodka and downed it quickly. Lowering the glass, a sense of relief passed across her face.

She moved closer and laid her head on his shoulder. They chatted briefly. He ate the remaining fries and coaxed her into eating a few more. As soon as he finished eating, he lit another cigarette. Silently, he put his arm around her. She nestled more tightly into his shoulder. As he finished the cigarette, they rose from their seats quietly and left.

He knew what she needed. He gave what she needed and what she wanted. Within the time it took me to eat, he grew taller and stronger – in charge of their lives, taking care of her.

She's a lucky girl. He will only love like that once.

**ANGELEE DEODHAR**

# Haiku Silence

So much has been written about how to haiku that I wonder if there is anything really left to say. More and more books on the art and craft of haiku are being written, and there are innumerable websites expressing opinions and publishing haiku by the score. Some of these are conflicting in content and leave even experienced poets bewildered.

For some time now, I have been asking myself the questions every haiku poet asks: Where does one begin? What is the quality of a good haiku? Does the fact that a haiku is published mean that it is a good one? What does a haiku really mean?

In my studies, covering nearly two decades, I have yet to understand a lot of things about haiku. Many people, venerable teachers and editors of prestigious haiku magazines, have written so much already. Is there anything I can add? Having thought about it, I felt I could share one insight, which for me, is the single most important affirmation towards a "haiku mind," if we can call it that.

In *The History of Haiku Vol. 1,* R.H. Blyth lists thirteen characteristics of the Zen state of mind required for the creation and appreciation of haiku: Selflessness, Loneliness, Grateful Acceptance, Wordlessness, Non-Intellectuality, Contradiction, Humor, Freedom, Non-Morality, Simplicity, Materiality, Love and Courage. Not being a follower of Zen, I don't know if I can add anything to this exhaustive list. Tom Clausen, in his fine essay "A Haiku Way of Life," lists his own additional thirteen characteristics: Faith, Sharing, Discipline, Concision, Solitude, Humility, Awareness, Ritual, Creativity, Centering, Truthfulness, Curiosity and Patience. I am sure most of us have some criteria we can add to these lists. One does not have to be a practitioner of Zen to write haiku. For me, these characteristics begin and end in what I term, "Haiku Silence."

The noise of the world drowns out so much. Most of us cannot leave home and set up residence near a pond as Thoreau did, but one can empathize with what he wrote. Most of us have jobs to attend to, classes to teach, bills to pay, meals to cook, meetings to attend, speeches to make. To experience silence and solitude, setting aside the baggage of negative connotations that may be associated with "non-doing", can be very challenging. How, then, do we shrug off all of this and write haiku? By returning to silence. By going on a journey deep within ourselves, to a safe quiet place where the winds and gusts of everyday affairs do not trouble us, where we can find our own inner natures in tune with the nature around us. Silence is not the absence of sound; by listening with one's whole being, one can discover the silence within.

Dr. Eric Amman, in describing haiku, used the term "wordless poem". If something is wordless, how do we communicate it? How do we convey the depth of feeling of that particular moment to someone far away in time and place? How then does a haiku, the wordless poem, work when put into words? Let us examine one of his own poems which leaves so much unsaid . . .

*The names of the dead*
*sinking deeper and deeper*
*into the red leaves*
—Eric Amman, *The Haiku Anthology*

Can haiku silence be expressed? Yes! Whenever I read a haiku that resonates for me, I ask myself, where did this originate? How has the person communicated such quietude almost wordlessly? I will illustrate with two examples:

*summer stillness*
*the play of light and shadow*
*on the wind chimes*
—Peggy Willis Lyles, *The Haiku Anthology*

*Quiet afternoon:*
*water shadows*
*on the pine bark*
—Anita Virgil, *The Haiku Anthology*

Let us look at another example:
*Stillness sand*
*sifts through the roots*
*of a fallen tree*
—Con Van Dan Heuvel, *The Haiku Anthology*

Here we can actually see how these haiku work. There is a silent communion of peace in which, because of the poets' stillness, we pause and beauty pervades our consciousness. The play of light on wind chimes, shadows on the bark of the tree, and sand sifting through the roots of the fallen tree bring to us timeless images.

*another year*
*the tallest trees shade*
*the oldest headstones*
—DeVar Dahl, Volume XVII, June 2004, *Haiku Canada Newsletter*

Stillness is a prerequisite for any creative art, but moreso for haiku. It is interesting to note that although Basho was a renku master, he frequently went away to find himself. Was his journey to the interior just a travelogue, or was it more? Here are three excellent examples of tranquility and quietude, in the spirit of Basho:

*Summer trickles*
*noiselessly down*
*the moss-covered stone*
—Christopher Herold, *a path in the garden*

*from winter storage*
*the prow of a canoe*
*entering sunlight*
—Jerry Kilbride, *The Haiku Anthology*

*morning bird song–*
*my paddle slips*
*into its reflection*
—Michael Dylan Welch, *The Haiku Anthology*

Most of us are too busy churning out haiku, trying to get published in one journal or another, sending in entries to contests or posting to various lists. It amazes me to see such frenetic activity. I agree with Zinovy Vayman when he writes,

*On my palm*
*a lifeline wrinkled*
*with future deadlines*
—Zinovy Vayman, *Modern Haiku*, Vol. XXXIII, No. 1, Winter-Spring, 2002

While it is good to learn by exchanging ideas about how to write better haiku and join discussion groups, for me the main aim of writing haiku is to get to the center of my silence. Although that silence may well be interrupted . . .

*time to quit*
*I hear the bell*
*before the bell*
—LeRoy Gorman, *Modern Haiku,* Vol.33.2, Summer 2002

*silent prayer –*
*the quiet humming*
*of the ceiling fan*
—Lee Gurga, *The Haiku Anthology*

Does it mean that we should become hermits? No, not necessarily, but what will help is to develop a special quality of silent communion with oneself. Before we start to put pen to paper, we must get quiet. It does not matter if we are commuting on a train, waiting in a doctor's office, or at the airport. To write well, we must bring our conscious selves into a state of silent graceful acceptance of everything around us. Here is a haiku which qualifies what I mean.

*desert spring –*
*nothing, nothing in the world*
*but this full moon*
—William J. Higginson, *Modern Haiku,* Vol.33.2, Summer 2002

The late Robert Spiess, a long-time editor of *Modern Haiku*, wrote in his *Speculations,* "Another reason for the brevity of haiku is that the more words the more distance, the more silence the more proximity."

With just a few words, Harter, Clausen and Swede have skillfully captured that noiselessness in their haiku,

*meteor shower –*
*the glimmer*
*of the surf*
—*Penny Harter, Modern Haiku, Vol.33.2, Summer 2002*


*once*
*everyone is gone . . .*
*the clock*
—Tom Clausen, *Albatross*, Vol. V, No. 1, 1996


*alone at last*
*i wonder where*
*everyone is*
—George Swede, *The Haiku Anthology*


Spiess also cautions us, "Chuang Tzu said, 'If you have insight, you use your inner eye, your inner ear, to pierce to the heart of things, and have no need of intellective knowledge.' This is how haiku poets should proceed in their endeavours."

*abandoned garden –*
*following the scent*
*of the hidden jasmine*
— Ion Codrescu, *Mountain Voices*


*the long night . . .*
*a light rain beats time*
*on the cook pots*
— Jim Kacian, *Albatross*, Vol. VII, No. 2, 1998

*quiet evening,*
*a spider moves its shadow*
*across the wall*
—Tom Clausen, *Albatross*, Vol. VII, No. 2, 1998

The great Indian sage Sri Ramana Maharshi said: "Silence is never-ending speech. Vocal speech obstructs the other speech of silence. In silence one is in intimate contact with the surroundings. Language is only a medium for communicating one's thoughts to another. Silence is ever speaking."

How well this is illustrated in this haiku:

*temple yard*
*the sound*
*of stone buddhas*
—Stanford M. Forrester, *still*, Vol.5, No.2, Spring 2001

Here the poet is at peace with himself, with his surroundings, with the world at large. In that silence, he too becomes a buddha. In the next haiku, we experience tranquility:

*silence*
*the snow-covered rock*
*under winter stars*
—Bruce Ross, *The Haiku Anthology*

Let us go deep into our own space to discover what it is that we belong to:

*ikebana*
*the space*
*where the lily was*
—Pamela Miller Ness, from the leaflet *where the lily was*

One must embrace silence and solitude to realize its full potential. In the next two haiku, feel yourself sinking into deep tranquility:

*deep in this world*
*of Monet water lilies . . .*
*no sound*
—Elizabeth Searle Lamb, *Across the Windharp, Collected and New haiku*

*marble koi . . .*
*the silence of*
*lotus blossoms*
—Pamela A. Babusci, *Evergreen*, Vol. X111, No. 5, May 2003

How can we fully feel a moment's essence if the mind is jumping from one thought to another? In a state of alertness, true awareness cannot occur unless we are in a mode of stillness. John Stevenson's haiku puts it so succinctly:

*a useless novelty –*
*each of us already has*
*a chattering skull*
—John Stevenson, *Modern Haiku*, Vol. XXXII, No. 1 Winter-Spring 2001

Recently, on one of the *kukai* lists of which I am a member, I wrote to the webmaster and said that this time, none of the haiku impressed me or brought an `aha!' moment. He gently reminded me that our response depends upon what we bring to a haiku. What a revelation! I had used my chattering skull instead of my silent self and missed appreciating the haiku. The reading of haiku and their appreciation also requires an alert passivity.

I end with a haiku that I keep on my table to remind me to write in such a manner that I (the host) can, through haiku, share with you (my guest) the pure silence of the white chrysanthemum . . .
*Silent communion*
*Between the guest, the host,*
*and the white chrysanthemum*
—Oshima Ryota

**REFERENCES CITED:**

1. *The Haiku Anthology*, Cor van den Heuvel, ed. 3rd ed (1999: W.W. Norton)
2. *Classic Haiku, A Master's Selection*, selected and translated by Yuzuru Miura. (1999: Charles E. Tuttle Company, Inc.)
3. *Mountain Voices*, Ion Codrescu. (2000: AMI-NET International Press).
4. *Across the Windharp*, Elizabeth Searle Lamb. (1999: La Alameda Press)
5. *A Year's Speculations on Haiku*, Robert Spiess, *Modern Haiku*, 1995.
6. Elizabeth St. Jacques website "In the Light," for Tom Clausen's essay, "A Haiku way of Life"

poetry

**DAVID AMRAM**

# For Neal Cassady on His Birthday

*(Read by his son John at the suggestion of his sister Jami for the First Annual Neal Cassady Birthday Bash at My Brother's Bar in Denver, Colorado, Sunday, Feb. 7, 2010)*

Here we are in Denver

a city that's for real

and no matter what goes down

we're all gathered here for Neal

we only have his memory now

he's in another place

he left town quite a while ago

to find another space

I saw him last in '65

and spent some really happy days

and fun-filled nights in San Francisco

then we went our separate ways

"you're thirty-four you're getting old Dave

when will you slow down"?

"Neal, like you I never will

as long as I'm around"

"Well Dave the next time you see Jack

please tell him you saw ol' Neal

and that I miss him everyday

that's how I really feel

The world's gone nuts and passed us by
made me look like a clown
but there's still kids who read Jack's books
and know what's going down.
I'll get my own books out some day
I'll tell the world my story
and share all those untold tales
of the power and the glory
Of old friends and long gone places
all the towns I traveled to
with my brakeman's shining lantern
lighting up the morning dew
the next time I see you
we'll sing "Pull My Daisy" once  again
whenever and wherever
I can hardly wait til then"
Well that "then" never happened
after nineteen sixty five
those were the final days and nights
the last year I saw Neal alive
but now in Denver he's come back
to visit us again
to tell us stories like he always
thrilled us with back then
of crazy nights in Five Points
and the saints of Larrimer Street

who sang their songs and shared their wine

and searched for food to eat

And how he married Carolyn

and started a new life

with their three angelic children

and his perfect wife

i wrote this poem for his son John

to read to all of you tonight

Like all of you I think of Neal

and his lantern shining bright

And how his spirit like that brakeman's lantern

fills the world with light

to light the way for all of us

to show us how to do it right

'cause doing right is what he did

and what we all must do

each day to share our dreams and blessings

long before our lives are through

So for our dear Carolyn

in Bracknell England far away

and for all his family here tonight

and friends across the USA

Let's tip a glass for Neal tonight

Wish i were here to play my horn

in the streets of downtown Denver

not far from where Neal was born

Hope next year while on that endless road
that i'm still traveling on
I'll be with all of you in Denver
so that i can sing along
i send love through my main man John
to celebrate with all of you
this birthday for your native son
and know that when the evening's through
you'll see a soft glow in the sky
in the Denver Rockies night
and know that Neal's still here with you
his brakeman's lantern shining bright

**JOHN VINCENT ROULEAU**

# Winter Storms

As another Pacific winter storm rolls into Northern California, with its grey omnipresence, my mind drifts back to the cabin I shared with my brother on Trout Brook outside Hudson, WI. Throughout the winter, embers glimmered in the limestone fireplace while two young men solved the world's problems. Darkness fell in the early evening. Life, you are sacred.

1.

New shadows close
a sunny day;
new rain soon
to follow

for a change.

Three years of drought
and we don't quite
trust winter anymore,

like an unfaithful lover.

2.

On radar for days
I watch it
march across the ocean,
northward and warm
from Polynesia,
southeasterly and cold
from the Gulf
of Alaska.

winter / spring 2011

My aching winter soul
waits, anxious and yearning
for winter's liquid kiss.

3.

Five days
from last rain

It fell for days in sheets

A wet kiss
to awaken summer sleeping
grasses, cause
that certain tingle
way
down

in the roots

Up
POP
tender green
new year
shoots

4.

Rain and more rain!

Summer's half-empty reservoirs
drink like thirsty sailors, remembering
drought.
If only for now,
winter's cup runneth over.

5.

rain falls when it will
unconcerned with drought or flood
wise men claim high ground

6.

drink now thirsty land
winter rain doth yield too soon
summer forsakes thee

7.

no birds for a week
feeders full, dripping with rain
fires in the fireplace

8.

Typically,
there'd be more people complaining,
what with

five weeks of rain.

But that's not the case.

We've learned a lot
about shortages lately,
of jobs, of hope, of peace,

of water.

We're grateful now
for every blessing, and pray
for more.

KATE HARDING

# Spring After a Long Cold Berkeley Winter

*for Olivia*

My old four cylinder Pontiac Tempest climbing
green, velour Berkeley hills. Your fiancé, my father
both in jails down south. Plum trees in bloom.
The latest New Directions in our scuffed purses.
Chanting "To a Poor Old Woman," "Rip Rap,"
"Howl," we cruise down dark, tree lined streets past
Van Gogh irises, roses in bloom. One of the ivy-
covered bungalows could be Rexroth's or Ginsberg's.

Ginsberg, wild curls, wild arms, words like waves,
a nervous shepherd directing his flock on Telegraph.
You in a pea-green yellow check maternity dress.
The two of us standing in shadows at the curb.

My waitress, your secretary money running out.
Our apartment on Ashby. The oven door that never
closed. The window that never opened. Strawberries
from the co-op. Spiral notebooks with UC Berkeley

on the covers. We wrote all that spring. In love with
William Carlos Williams, his plums, his nasturtiums,
his asphodel, his white space. Our poems, footprints
on the page, we said. Seagull tracks across the sand.

Our hair neatly combed, shoes polished, we slid past
Sather Gate. We pretended we were UC students
sneaked into the back of Thom Gunn's poetry class.
The real students, girls from good homes, hawk nests
hair, torn blue jeans, were dropping out. We were
slipping in.

**KATE HARDING**

# Reading Po Chu'i on a Rainy Night
# I Dance Sometimes

My belly too full, the night
late, I read Po Chu'i who after
collecting taxes in autumn
from peasants he loved
drank too much wine
and danced sometimes.

My own shopping cart
full, I give a quarter
to the woman with whiskey
on her breath, a dusty black
poodle and an old rag coat
and empty cans in her cart
on a cold Saturday night.
I drink too much wine
and dance sometimes.

Men far from their home
in Mexico, live next to me
in shacks, with cloths for
windows, and rain leaking in.
They pick avocados
I lace with lime and cilantro.
I drink too much wine
and dance sometimes.

Dawn to dark,
young girls in Viet Nam,
necks curled like old women,
straw cutting their fingers
weave beach mats
I sit on in summer.
I drink too much wine
and dance sometimes.

# How You Began

*for Danny*

The front of the year.
Your father and I.
A soft night in a little
back house on Raymond.

Neighbor children, Susie,
Karen, Steve safe in bed
for the night.

A love song in Spanish
from the cottage across
the street. Enrique's
cigarette glowing
under the avocado tree.

Love, ripe like the oranges,
lanterns in the trees.
You were made in Ocean Park
at the beginning of the year.

The sea, a skein of gold
five city blocks away
under a full moon.

The trolley with lights
and bells
trundling up the boardwalk.

Women in babushkas,
men in prayer shawls.
Bonfires on the beach.

Ukuleles and bongos.
Poets and junkies seeing
magic in the flames.

You began in the bedroom
with the slanted roof.
Yellow oxalis
blooming wild at our door.

**R.T. SEDGWICK**

# The Moon is a Stone Gone Mad

*—after Richard Shelton*

All the stones
on the hill
feel its pull

the elder stones
their younger sons
stones of the night

whispering white stones
sedentary stones
stones of age and youth

but the old stones won't budge
as their young seek out streams
to move them like small moons

old stones won't follow the moon
content to stay where they are
sit on their butts and grow moss

when the young fall asleep
the old stones talk of sins
conjured up from their past

sins of when they roamed
they themselves gone mad
like the moon they strayed

now it's their turn
to teach the young
about the moon

all the stones
on the hill
feel its pull

**GARY LAWLESS**

# I Asked the Fox

I asked the fox to
speak to you,
in your dreams.
He said there are
universes and universes,
stars move stars
move, everything
has another name.
I asked the fox to
tell me your name.

# eel poem

water, and how it
makes its way, dreaming
of eels, moving
in darkness, below,
below water, moving
eels in darkness,
dreaming darkness,
eel water.

climbing the mountain,
above the valley,
above the clouds
Sunday morning greeted by
red spotted newt,
we bow and pass by,
leaving everything
behind

RYKA AOKI

# Indigenous

I looked out my window.
Academics were putting theories into practice—
berating the gardeners—
saying planting anything here was stupid.
Nothing grows here that doesn't need water.

My friend felt homeless. He didn't want shelter.
He wanted a Real City.
I said find an all-night noodle place
that serves fish sauce in salty glass bottles.
He asked, "Can they make the food
without pork, or chili, or MSG?"

There's a story about the palm trees—
how they arrived one day in air-cushioned truck beds
summoned from central casting
for movie stars, golf courses and poolside bungalows.

Some trees escaped and went feral.
If you're quiet, you can hear them trying to recall
what they looked like before they were forced
to lose weight and get boob jobs.

That's the story most of you believe.
But last weekend I found there's one type of palm tree
indigenous to Los Angeles. It's never been caught.

It's on the down low, disguised
as an immigrant local, or another freeway
transplant.

I think I heard it sing tagalog karaoke.
I think I saw it sell a bag of cherries.
I heard it teaches shaolin kung fu in the basement
of an El Monte apartment, and on weekends
serves the best menudo in town.

If my friends would understand me,
I would tell them. But all they'd say
is that it's only one type of tree.
And they would never hear me say
I know, but one is all we need.

RYKA AOKI

# Oh, Sons of Adam!

It is not that we have no names.
Your tongue does not curl its consonants,
nor loft its vowels forward and back.

Your alveola does not evoke the Altjeringa.
You ear cannot shift between 妈 and 馬,
to hear *mother*, then *horse*.

You may know Everything.
But you do not know everything.
You cannot say our names.
So you remove our names.

For in your Everything, what you cannot
is *not*.

Yet we shall sing to our children anyway—
of highlands, oceans, mountains on fire, anyway.

For other songs shelter the heart
—of hauki, jabu, tinikling, and uyot. Love
weaves souls amongst other grasslands
and islands and ice.

And when a newborn cries
and you cannot hear why,
Know the child, the child knows of ayame
and acaxochitl, of sarangerel, and hrefna.

Of the names we forsook
when your tongues entered us,
silenced us, then bade us
come.

CLIFTON KING

# Buffalo

I am Buffalo.
In the days after the first moon
I was thunder across the prairies,
a pageant of dust that settled on the sun.
I was as many as the blades of grass.
The earth trembled beneath my hooves.
Long before this land had a name
the Indian came and we were brothers.
He took what he needed, nothing more.

I am Buffalo.
My brother danced and sang my name
in his lodge, painted his face for the hunt.
I gave myself: my flesh for food, my hide
for warmth, my bones for tools.
Glorious death, then, I lived forever in legend.
Buffalo. I was revered

— until the Anglo.
You came with horses and guns,
your ignorance and greed.
I ran from your bullets but you killed me
again and again,
ripped the hide from my carcass,
left my flesh to rot in the sun,
prairie red with blood,
the stench of slaughter.

You killed me to starve the Indian.
You killed me for sport
from your iron horse.
You killed me and laughed,

to impress a woman,
to win a bet, to pass the time.
You murdered me
and never gave it a thought.

I am Buffalo.
Never again will the thunder be heard,
the earth tremble, the sun fade
in the sod churned by multitudes.
Now you struggle to rescue me
from your own hand.

I am Buffalo.
Back from the grave,
the mountains of bleached bones,
back from the slaughter.

Not because I am revered.
Not because we are brothers.
But, because you are ashamed.

CLIFTON KING

# Vestido Rojo

On a beach in Manzanillo, Mexico
fishing boats lie overturned, lined up
like contestants in a beauty contest.
Pulled high on the sand to avoid tides
they soak up a fresh coat of paint.
Blue a favorite color, the same hue
as a cloudless summer sky. Others, green
as chili verde served at Carmen's Cantina.

I find a place in the shade,
watch fishermen repair their nets,
share stories of the sea. I know a poem
is somewhere among these faces,
weather worn hands, sheen of wet paint.

Beyond the boats, a woman walks
at water's edge, shoes in hand.
A red dress hugs her ample hips,
reveals cleavage of such proportions
a careless lover might be lost forever
in its depths. I came to write about
these boats. Yet, just as the bull cannot
control his charge at the matador's cape,
I leave the fishermen to their chores,
chase after that woman in the red dress.

TIMOTHY DEAN MARTIN

# flinch

1.
the destruction was
beyond insurance; but i lived
there no more/
claims were only carved
against the vacant/ time was in
the wind/ past was
passed/ torn, mended;
lost, found/
broken hearts transplanted
with a common sense savoir-faire/

and yet just as sure
as a getaway,
there are those collectors
who never give up/
whose soul occupation
is teaching us to recall;
to flinch
just in case/

and testify
that memories bleed/

2.
half of life is night;
we paint our own dark/
nothing covers our shadows
except broad brushstrokes
and stillness/
we stand
back to the nearest exits/
face trying
not to twitch
and give ourselves away/
but we must;
and again/

3.
i created what hunts me
in the night;
it leaps like a light switch
on my insecurities,
eating my confidence/now
i lay me down,
and there is no sleep/

i father my weakness;
raised by the accusation
of terrible mistakes/
i gasp in anticipation
of my missteps/ nothing seems
to disappear in a thousand good deeds/
the scars are shaped like a lifetime;
the tears forever,
the night too long/

4.
it didn't come all at once
like most thoughts in flashes when i
let them/ it was like cats feet on my first
waking/ i almost didn't know
until i did; and then
a slow denying shrug
of shoulders followed by a flinch
that knew something was there/
something that glimpsed back,
a thing that noticed
and waited its turn patiently/
for me to change it
into lines each metered
and timed like the mathematics
of pain;
like the poems torn up
lest the truth escape to strangers/

now it draws me,
it asks to be introduced/
i must
as I am unfortunately too polite
and its dread needs to be fed;
this unpainted guest
at the last supper/

this ungrateful unwanted uninitiated
unkind unfortunate
end;
announcing
itself in the whisper
of my own voice/

5.
the house is no more,
but the ghost is real/
they built a freeway over it
and cars whiz through
my old living room/ it was
doomed to repeat itself;
a broken record of dysfunctional
harmony/ i've kept moving
until there are no more rooms,
kept flinching
until the palsied past
has left me shaken/
and all that's left
is knowing that
things break/
night's dark/
best isn't always/
truth is/

**THEA IBERALL**

# When Civilizations Die

*Dedicated to Otto "Professor Offtop" Pearson 1946-1992*

My almanac lists the great ones: Babylonians, Romans, Greeks—
freedancing fools, like you, hung by history.

Did Aristotle know the republic was dying:
did Thalia take flight? As Thebes flourished,
did Socrates sense the cadence
faltering as poets conjured empty rhymes
and drumming foot soldiers collapsed to their knees
vanquished by Persians and smallpox,
their campfires spent under our canopy of stars,
a civilization lost, a time left silent, gone
like Naomi to Moab, disappearing like the hanging
gardens of Babylon, the powerful sword of a proud
Athenian people spread too thin to repel the Spartans in one
too many sea battles in the Peloponnesian War?

Was Caesar Augustus aware of his destiny? Roman Empire
expanding, barges flush with Spanish wine, Egyptian grain,
bubonic plague, to be done in by the lead in their drinking cups
and the Franks caracoling at their border?
No more Caesar. Gone the weight of a million marching feet
across the scorched Tiberian plain swept under the corded rug of
time.

And does civilization's death begin with the fools?
Is it the clowns that go first, like you, dead
by insidious exploding cells popping
bulges behind your white mask, dead
by one too many magic tricks, dead
by your own hand at the rope, your public's laughter

spent staring mindlessly at our canopy of stars,
a civilization lost, a time left silent, toes
defying gravity, pointed slightly inwards.

Civilizations grow from seed to shaft.
When you took to the rope, did you find the lost civilization
the one left between the lines at MacDonalds the one
we cling to like Ruth to Naomi *whither thou goest, I will go*
but you took to the rope you reached for Babylon
left the poets conjuring empty rhymes,
       people having conversations but never talking
       we meet we exchange pager numbers
       favorite ethnic restaurants but when do we say I can't go
       on?
       I don't need another twenty-three minute sitcom
       to make me feel better. When you took to the rope
       do you know you took the best from my canopy of stars,
       leaving a civilization lost, a time left silent, Thalia dead.

There is no peace for civilization, it surrounds us
like a mother's womb, the endless drum night
after night, year after year extinct like aching
twine, infinite stretches of time
disappearing in an eyeblink
a disease eating away from the inside
we each have our own Peloponnesian War.

THEA IBERALL

# Friday Night at Agios Konstantinos

The big event is the evening stroll
down the uneven street, homes

not twenty feet from the Aegean
watered by church and woods,

house-front walls a backdrop
for old faces staring

out to sea, waiting for sons
from wars and daughters

with babies. Couples tilt drinks
at Heaven's Bar, lovers huddle

under boulders on the beach.
Smoke dries around backgammon

men leathered at the Kafeneio
as the sea womb tightens

on families mid-bite
in tavernas open to the air.

Curious eyes these humans have,
following darkness and each other.

They watch as movements mew into form
knowing the sea is there,

listening to the footsteps,
the blinking trees, the smell of the air.

MAI LON GITTELSOHN

# Chinatown – Yesterday, Today

How to describe the Chinatown of my youth
captured as it is in the mind of a child
who cannot control where or when to go,
but can only hold onto her mother's hand
or stumble after her sisters, who are wearing
too much make-up, her father striding ahead,
while her mother follows
almost at his side.

Roast ducks hang by their trussed legs
in the window of the poultry shop, eyes
like slits, oval nostrils in the beak dark
craters on the moon, bronzed skin
dripping fat.

Fog horns bleat as mist settles gently
around our shoulders; I feel the press
of bodies, families with children, gray-haired ladies
carrying oranges in string bags, lips clamped tight
after a day at the sewing factory pushing fabric
under the wicked flash of needles.

Everywhere the lonely Chinese bachelor
reading the Chinese newspaper
on the corner of Grant and Stockton,
in the window of Uncle H's coffee shop
sipping coffee with a slab of apple pie,
climbing four flights of narrow steps
to swallow rice porridge at night, letting the soup
bland and gelatinous, slide down his throat,
sore from too many cigarettes.

Today, a visit to Chinatown is a trip to Hollywood –
desperate hostesses dressed in silk
stand in doorways waving menus–
*Come in! Come in!*
*Try our authentic Chinese food.  No Chop Suey.*
Tourists find toys made in Vietnam
while I keep looking for my past,
past the stone lions
guarding the gateway
to a deserted Grant Avenue.

NELLY WILLIAMS

# She Jane, Me Tarzan
# (The Story of Petra)

The most beautiful thing about Petra was
Her lower lip.  So red!  So full!
I loved Petra.
I loved to watch her back and forth around the house
Swinging wide hips from side-to-side
Big belly up front.

Her family had thrown her out.
My family had rescued her,
For Petra had become encinta
From a boy named el sinverguenza,
(That's what everybody called him at the time.)
Later on I learned that this meant he was a scoundrel—
That he had no shame.

The most beautiful thing about Petra was
The dress she wore:
A loose white habit with long sleeves—
Just like a nun's, but with no headdress.
And a long brown rope around her waist
Due to a promise she had made to the Virgin Mary
To perform that sacrifice until the father of her unborn child
Returned to her.

The most beautiful thing about Petra,
According to the blacksmith's son, was
That she never wore panties.
This for sure I did not know, but once in a while
I would see him and his friends, crouched under our house,
Looking up through a crack on the kitchen floor,
Where Petra stood to cook our meals.

The most beautiful thing about Petra was
She loved to steal.
And I, at eight, loved to watch when she did this:
I loved to watch when she took money from my family's suitcase,
Which my mother and my father thought was safe,
Hidden, under their bed.

The most beautiful thing about Petra was her kindness.
She gave my mother a long gold chain,
Which she bought with my mother's money.
(This, my mother did not know, so my mother was delighted!)
She did not have the chain for long,
For the long chain soon disappeared.
Poof!  Petra gave it to someone else,
As Petra was inclined to do.

The most beautiful thing about Petra was
Her perfect teeth, her perfect smile, the two dimples on her cheeks,
Her long blonde hair, her taste in shoes—never high heels—
Only soft wedgies.
"The better to sneak into a friend's house, my dear."
And sure enough, from one of them she stole . . . a bracelet!
(And although I was a boy of eight I wished I had a bracelet too.)

The most beautiful thing about Petra was
When on Saturday nights, holding my hand
She would take me to el meaito,
A movie theater around the corner from our house,
Where, in the darkness, rolling up a sleeve,
She would expose:  The rhinestone bracelet!

> Circle of tiny flashing lights
> Reflecting colors from the screen
> Equal to the stars outside

There, at el meaito Petra and I
Would eat popcorn, watch the news of the war,

See coming attractions, cartoons, episodes . . .
Plus a film on zombies, mummies, wolf men,
King Kong, Frankenstein.
Or,
Jane and Tarzan.
All for the 25 cents that once a week Petra would steal,
The most wonderful thing Petra ever did.

*encinta = pregnant*
*sinverguenza = shameless*
*el meaito = a cheap movie house*

# A Consideration of Lightning

### I

"Consider lightning," you wrote, so I did,
hesitantly, haltingly, in stark segments
as it slashed all around, striking ground

with a vehemence bordering on vengeance,
as if directed by some fiery hand,
some god with whom I'd dared to disagree.

I considered it rationally,
then stepped into the screaming bolt,
steeled my lightning legs, and vaporized

light itself. A darkness slapped to ground,
suffocating every twinkling thing,
every sparkling thing, every warmth

a foul cessation, a lack so immediate
that I wondered *Wait! Wasn't that space filled
just a moment ago with blazing heat?*

### II

*Consider lightning....* My moment was done
and my core chilled, though I tried anxiously
to grasp the fleeting memory as we,

lightning and I, mimicked each other,
took turns striking, searing, sizzling—
but my heart wasn't in it. I remained

in awe of that bold heat, that piercing flash,
the agony of all that purity,
the frigid, stifled darkness the lightning brought

strapped to its electric underbelly,
slouching, gelid, heavy darkness curdled
amidst the cold, bone-drenching rain.

## III

*Consider lightning....* It's easier to strike
from here in the heavens to the ground
quickly, painfully, screaming down like fire

on a rail. You know, the weatherman
tries to explain in human terms
why you shouldn't stand beneath a tree

to hide from lightning strikes or in the middle
of a field, your nine iron at the apex
of your swing, defiantly, for grins.

But fire and ice in the speed of light
cannot be explained in human terms.
It's like flash attachments going off

at a soccer game that gets rained out,
with fans and gamers running from the field
as god snaps angry pictures. Anyway,

none of this explains the lightning mind,
the migraine raised to a form of art,
how not-mortal it is. Despite science

and weathermen with little triangles
and maps, lightning has nothing to do
with electromagnetics. I know that now.

I've seen the gods get angry, seen the curtain
rent, seen the godly plasma flash
a million times an instant, heaven to earth,

a tiny fit, a spasmodic release
of pent-up godly steam, fending off
another flood... for now.

**HARVEY STANBROUGH**

# Beyond the Masks

*from and for Gerald Whitefoot St. Clair, just a man*

> *"There used to be gods in everything*
> *and now they've gone...."*
> ~ Howard Nemerov in "The Companions"

**I**

Before we lost the gods or sight of them
and let them fade away beyond the masks

that separate their world (*the* world) and us,
we knew there was a line between the sea

and the coral resting there; between
the stream and the rocks that line its bed;

between the liquid and the bowl; between
the fruit and the seed; between the void

and the atmosphere; and between
the music and the flute. We heard the gods

in creaking branches, in the touch of rain,
and consequential gatherings of birds,

their flappings tuned perfection to the ear
their song an invocation in the trees,

whence they would rise as one to form a sign
then turn this way and that, as if on signal,

before they settled to the trees again
to talk excitedly among themselves

about the gods they'd called, whether those gods
would visit them and us ever again.

## II

I walk with you to look beyond the masks,
to see us as we were before The Fall,

before we lost the ears to hear the gods
in everything, before we lost the eyes

to see the gods, the sense to know their worth.
I walk with you to taste the sweet mesquite,

the silence layering the land, the music
trickling down the Rio Peñasco;

I walk with you to smell the dusty sage
just before it rains, the joyful sage

just afterward, and to know a god
made the difference; and I walk with you

to learn to count the threads in mescal,
listen for a blessing on the wind,

and watch a single grain of dust settle
gently on a yellowed blade of grass.

## III

Before we slipped beyond the masks, the gods
guided us, beheld our gangly stride,

our awkward gait as if we hadn't grown
into our feet. They watched us flail about,

feigning all the while a certain status,
lifting ourselves even over them

until we couldn't hear them when they spoke
and so they fell silent. But now I walk

with you to hear them creak in juniper,
see them hunched beside the craggy rocks,

and know that we and they are of one heart,
the rhythmic heartbeat of the Law of One

as if they'd never gone, as if we'd never
turned our backs on them in our headlong

rush to leave ourselves behind, our rush
to be who we are not. But now we know:

We listen to the earth and to the gods.
We hear them and we see them peeking at us.

They slip across the window pane at night,
they whisper softly just outside the door,

and sometimes, when I've been well behaved,
they rustle dust in moonbeams on my desk.

MARTE BROEHM

# I'm Not Manzanita, Roots Set into Crags and Rock

I am morning as the crows fly east, I am morning in a gray tree line before the sun is out of bed, I am morning just waiting to rise.

I understand the rabbit in the garden, why she avoids dieffenbachia, why she digs a hole beneath bougainvillea, how she's survived so many months alone.

I want to drop into the palm of Yosemite Valley, follow its river like a life-line, climb its Venus mount beneath a glacier rock's thumb.

I would like to live in North Fork, a wood cabin among winding roads, rocks, forest, and there below a hill covered by cypress, a splashing stream.

I understand how John could do it, John, gone so long, too soon, even though he told me it was time, but I can't help missing him.

I would like to be Peckinpah Mountain, how it rises up beneath the pitch of absolute night, reaching for winking stars above my head, too many to count.

I am the kiss blown into the wind from a child's open hand, I am those lips pushed together after fingers wiggle saying good-bye.

I wish I could bob, break over trunks of fallen trees, gush over boulders making them smooth, ramble, no hint of a face or its dried salt.

I can be soft like the subdued voice of Jimi Hendrix as the *wind cries Mary,* I can be the fling of strings in a *purple haze*, but my father loves these things about me.

I could be a needle embroidering, could move in-and-out, lay a smooth satin stitch, fill-in birds on dishtowels, or fatten letters in names on stockings.

I don't want to be brows frowning, or a mouth saddled down, but let me be warm arms pulling you in, saying, *Here you are.*

I don't understand how to rage a holy-war, nor Bin Laden's call for suicide, yet I can imagine intentions twisting to fanatical, how a cause becomes insane.

I'd like to be a small rainbow fading below the rail of a cabin deck, not the puddle beside it in cold mud, not the bare wooden step, creaking.

I would love to be morning fog above a gorge, a soft pillow in the crater of lake, but not the dampness, not a tissue full of tears.

I am fading, becoming my mother's words as she speaks in the dark, the hollow hall, that echo on stairs too steep to run, I am a shoulder, the apron and bread.

# Starlings

A starling's warblings wakes my dawn,
singing me into dusky memories of
that drawer beneath the linen closet,
the one that would never quite close,
stuffed with wrinkled sheets of
my sister's written warblings.

I'd awaken to a starling's and
my sister's songs.
I'd awaken to the serenade of a smile
on the pillow next to mine.
I'd awaken to expectations for a morning critique.
Turning towards the wall was my sunrise response,
but
in the evening I'd crescent into her poetry.
She'd hum parts of her yet-to-be finished melodies,
sometimes even asking me for rhyme.
She'd weave my child-chatter into her music:
*I listen to the goodnight calls from the trees -*
*kissing slimy fish leaning over on my knees.*

She'd laugh -
Lyrics I still hear
whenever a starling sings.

KATHRYN KOPPLE

# Always With Whitman

I read his poems and don't care anymore who I might be.
If I am a woman let him paint my skirt bright as a yellow awning,
a canopy generous and swaying over supple hips,
or let him see that I am a man and he lies awake in bed with me
under a roof of polished beams,
the flicker of the lamp repeating in the windows.

And always I feel him close, his diction and intonation,
each syllable a chime struck against distress and solitude,
each cadence an ointment, a balm to soften resentment,
and deposit on my lips some earthy souvenir,

the ash that lingers on the tongue,
the nectar that washes it clean.

**HARRY GRISWOLD**

# Frying Pan Pantoum

We dodge thunderbolts the gods hurl
down upon us like nobody's business.
Preachers insist the gods above love us
even if life turns to bilk and money.

Down on us like nobody's business,
despite sweet tales we were told as kids,
we watch life turn to bilk and money.
Votes get sold, elections go up for bid,

all in spite of sweet tales we tell to kids.
Nearly everyone down here complains
when we see votes sold, elections up for bid,
and when attack is a campaign's backbone.

Almost everyone down here complains,
from mad aunts to my dreamy cousins,
big money backs those attack campaigns.
Some try to hide on the farm, disguised.

For mad aunts and dreamy cousins
it's blessed escape they pray for daily,
they'd love to hide on the farm, disguised
among fresh eggs and hens who laid them.

Escape is the answer they pray for daily
out where bees gather the gods' own nectar
far from bad eggs and pols who laid them.
We're offered elephant-mule savior games

while bees gather the gods' sweet nectar
and preachers insist those above love us.
First it's savior elephant, then savior mule,
and we dodge thunderbolts the gods hurl.

**HARRY GRISWOLD**

# RAGGEDY RIDER

Many have dropped away, including
the Kennedys, Martin, Malcolm, our
parents good or bad, God in many
forms and his buddy Santa. School
seemed safe but that was fake. Even
our sung-about oceans don't protect
America, and the poor preamble
to the Constitution floats adrift with
the rest of it. I've learned to hate
hot dogs, but I have good children
and they have theirs. Nothing ripped
away can change the early days —
Kraus and Fisher my best buddies,
Laurie Davis across the street biting
my arm, making it bleed in my first
exchange of bodily fluid. My words
won't make anyone care about the rocks
my life sits on, so let's turn, consider
yours. And is that a farm I see? Old
wholesome farms — where the Bible
was smoked most evenings. And kids
ran off to the city anyway, for sex, work,
for cutting ties to corn-based life.
Our overrun cities have rotted. Can we
make them whole again? As strong people
we bury bad marriages, abuses, the rigors
of imposed religion. We still sing to kids,
read them stories and let them laugh. Put

kids around dogs a lot and they'll know
a species not so beat up as our own.
I sit here under a fine pine tree, yet I
don't turn to look up, even if branches
above me touch, like our extended arms
could. Beyond, I ignore the vast blue
even though it keeps fish and all the rest
from flying wildly into space.

**LINDA ENGEL AMUNDSON**

# Geometry of Fog

Butter coated fingers
fondle small white breasts of dough
a white linen covers what will
rise for the day of the dead
a gift for our ghosts
greedy for sweets
the cigarettes and heat
of the living

You have moved beyond corruption
bone meal for the sycamores
and still I am greedy to feel your skin
slide against mine I need to smell
your sleeping breath soft
with the tang of goat's milk
to re-experience the terrifying first time
the fusion of our bodies

it wasn't always geometry
you taught me
on the windshield of your car
fogged with our
mingling breathe

LINDA ENGEL AMUNDSON

# Road to Perdition

*Zoom Zoom Zoom*

I pass Responsibility Rd. at 90

I sing as I sail on the casino highway

Mr. Jitters in a porkpie hat

polishes his plastic visa

my snakeskin boots walk me

to a spot sweet with luck

lights flash mellow bells trill

cardboard women

stare holes in their cards

beef jerky men

blink with one eye

wink with the other

*Zoom Zoom Zoom*

Listen to the music

Murder is about to play

sweaty glasses clink dice rattle

seven come eleven everyone loses

Fan Tan Pan Caribbean Poker

name your hemlock Sherlock

luck is in a hammock with a feather and fan

Mr. Bad Luck stands on the shoulders

of happy buffet eaters

gives the call *Hey Rube*

*come back sooner than later*

to shell out the dinero

*Zoom Zoom Zoom*

Girls in glass dresses offer to

rub bacon on Mr. Jitters

toes his nose runs his hands shake

to the rhythm of Xavier Cugat's band

left for dead when the old

Flamingo went up in a Portobello

dust cloud

*Zoom Zoom Zoom*

My silver studded jacket

woos the chips the dice roll my way

the Nuwavo Poor look bewildered

bled out luck shy

re-con ready marks

perforated wallets gasp for refills

luck jumped ship and headed

for China on Typhoon Juan

DICK EIDEN

# The Lesser of Two Evils,
# Or How I Swallowed the Cat

They're widening the freeway
      to forty-seven lanes, no shoulder
            to cry on, no even-handed dispensations

from jewel-encrusted statuary, smart phones
      set on stun, expect delays, hairballs
            in all directions, small bones evolved

into this ignorant, craven,
      depraved gridlock on Constitution
            Avenue, floating like a moth

in last night's red wine
      more numerous than enlightened
            alphabet soup of reasons why

cable chatter, vapid banter
      headlong slide into all-out
            food fight, late-night diversions

gearing down across yellow lines,
      another barren bailiwick
            heavens to Betsy

they've got us by the balls!

**TRISH DUGGER**

# Over the Edge

How easily we lose parts
of ourselves.
We move in and out of
each other like
shadows through statues,
leaving traces and
grabbing what we can
on this invisible odyssey.
While sliding through your
spine, I placed an ache
in your lower back
You took my sense of
balance when you
roamed inside my brain.
My heart gallops
across the moonscape
on your nightmare.
My mother, slightly tipsy,
walks inside me. I can't
find my mind anywhere.
An English woman
woke up one morning
with a French accent.
I speak in tongues.

**D.N. SUTTON**

# Question Mark

*(at age 90)*

If there is twilight
Have I asked it in
Have I myself suspended?

If there is twilight
I will face the night
Seek dawn
Hold firm against
My own offending
Knowing the never-ending
Promise of the noon.

If there is twilight
I will hang on intending
To embrace whatever
The impenetrable
Dark contains.

And when it wanes
I will stand in that half-light
Soft pale tones
Knowing in my gut, my bones
I will have earned, designed
This day.

My mind,
My most effective weapon
I can find
Will hold
Senseless fears
At bay.

I count on my gritty soul
To pronounce me whole
Hold on, sweet life
I am on my way!

**ANDREE STOLTE**

# Sweet Children of Tibet (Goodnight)

Sweet children of Tibet, goodnight
sleep lovely dear little ones
as white feathered wing sweeps over your exquisite dusty faces,
silent eyes

Gently touching your precious foot
dressed only in sock, dangling
then stroking lovely ashen mangled hair
and covering bare tummy
holding ever so softly, petit hand empty of doll or parent
reaching from the rubble
care not how Mothers red fluid sea stains your clothes
She has called you for her very own

I melt my form and place it in your tiny hand
And this heart
I have fallen before you, battered
Child angel
To catch you, cradle you
Caress your precious soul
My only bliss to carry you

And I'll tell your mommy that you are safe
and always were
fear not as you peer from the black velvet sky
your earth is new now
ablaze with primordial peace
kiss me goodnight and whisper to the wind
sweet dreams
and in the morning I shall take you to my playground

prose

**CHARLES REDNER**

# The Night BP Drove Old Dixie Down

Grandpa named her the *Lanai* after one of the Hawaiian Islands. She was a forty-four foot wooden-hulled sport fishing boat. Wasn't much to look at, but she provided for our family's livelihood for as long as I remember as we fished the bountiful and beautiful Gulf of Mexico.

A tributary of the Picayune River curls around our house and dock, which begins a twenty-minute cruise to the open waters of the Gulf. I've been fishing with Grandpa and Dad since I was high enough to jump over the gunnels. Lord, how I love the sea.

Last year on my sixteenth birthday, Dad gave me the lecture about college and made the case for earning a living outside fishing. I cut him off. Didn't want to hear it. Wouldn't consider it. Told him that this is the life for me. Dad quickly looked away, but I caught his smile.

Cancer took Mom in '95. Grandpa moved into the city with my aunt Ida after he fell and busted up his hip. Dad and I now live the good bachelor life, two fishermen whose only love is the memory of Mom, the sea, *Lanai*, and Maggie.

Maggie's our mascot, a big 'ol pelican that knows a good home when she finds one. Maggie's been coming around for months now. She's more loyal than a hound and twice as smart. Maggie's got a white battle scar across the very top of her beak, so we knew for sure that it's the same bird returning. She begins each morning perched on the far end of the dock, waiting for breakfast. As I approach, she spreads her massive wings and stretches that spiny neck skyward. I keep forgetting my camera—want a picture of that morning greeting for the family album.

Hot dogs. Maggie likes hot dogs best of all. Throw two toward her bucket-sized beak and the third just out of reach so she has to fish for the last one. After a few days, she began jumping into the water before I tossed the last dog. Like I said, smart bird.

Sky's dark this morning. Flags flapping straight out. Funeral weather. Won't be going out today, so I'll finish reading *Moby-Dick*.

Tomorrow, the weather's supposed to break. Hope so. Four oil rig guys have chartered the *Lanai* for a marlin hunt—best tasting thing to ever come out of the sea. Dad believes marlin run best at night, so we'll be going out after dinner. This'll be a first for me. I'm really pumped.

Promptly at seven, the oilmen drive up to our dock. They spill out of the truck laughing, joking while pulling on their cans of Bud.

My job is to help stow the gear, which consists mostly cases of beer and sandwiches which I load in the stern cooler. Dad fires up the twin Chryslers, I cast off the lines, and we chug away.

The oilmen claim they'd seen fins near their BP platform. After passing under Interstate 10 and clearing the marshes, we head south by southwest. A moonless night permits a full canopy of stars to blaze above.

Twenty miles out, a dim light appears over the port bow horizon. The image of a luminous island against a darkened world grows larger and brighter as we near. It's time to see that our guests are properly seated, strapped into their chairs. Dad throttles back and the boat slows. He shouts from the bridge for me to help bait and cast the lines.

After an hour of criss-crossing a four-mile area without luck, the oilmen ask Dad to go closer to their rig. With the lines in, Dad kicks her up and *Lanai* rises on plane with a jolt. We move within a few hundred yards of the rig.

The flash blinds me.

Night turns day. A thousand cannons roar. The blast knocks me on my ass. Fortunately, the bow points toward the platform or we'd be capsizing. Violent bobbing thrusts me against a rail.

Dad screams. He's fallen next to me. When he stands, his arm twists unnaturally behind him. He asks how I am. I read his lips and nod. I can't speak. He runs over to each oilman. They all seem okay. Dad climbs back up to the helm.

Just ahead, what had been a placid manmade island shatters in one gigantic, cataclysmic explosion that spawns an awesome inferno. Flames leap sixty feet into the blackness. A huge plume of smoke drifts toward us. It covers the *Lanai* in a putrid-smelling, eye-burning fog. I can't breathe.

Dad steers from the cloud. When our sight clears, all eyes turn to the battered rig. The silhouettes of workers run in every direction. Lifeboats drop from the rig. Abandoned riggers jump into the sea from the platform. I can't turn away. Too mesmerized by the horror. Dad yells at me, but my ears are ringing from the explosion. I can't make out a single word. He motions for me to unpack the life jackets. He heads for the burning rig.

The oilmen stand rigid, staring in disbelief, the shocked look of recent combat showing clearly on faces glowing pale orange from reflections of the furious fire.

We circle the platform, round and round, throwing life jackets at anything bobbing in the sea. We pull out the bloodied, the wounded, the already dead and the dying. Hours blend into a numbing blur. Fireboats shuttle in and out, trying to dampen the blaze. Flames easily gulp the sprays like thirsty oxen. Coast Guard ships join our effort to fish survivors out of the water.

With fuel low and little room left onboard, Dad steers for shore. The radio screeches with excited voices—some issuing instructions, others asking questions, still others screaming for help.

Two hours later, we spot the flashing lights of ambulances and maneuver to a New Orleans pier. Before we've completely tied up, EM personnel jump onboard and begin lifting the wounded ashore. Our oilmen help with the injured. I tie *Lanai* down and join Dad as he goes to the hospital to tend to his shoulder.

* * *

We wait for Dad's shoulder to heal, watch cable news and acknowledge the cancellation of previously booked dates. After two weeks, it doesn't matter, because the Environmental Protection Agency prohibits fishing in half of the Gulf nearest us. The news is constant, confusing and conflicted. Some say the spill effects will be minimal. Others declare it the worst environmental disaster in U.S. history.

At least Maggie comes back for her breakfast every morning. One day, I notice her feet are brownish. That same day, the odor of oil begins to flare our nostrils and the water surface takes on a purplish sheen.

Maggie stops coming around.

Weeks turn into months. Still the oil pours out of the well. Even the president's command to, "Stop the damn leak!" cannot be obeyed. With our business shut down and the likelihood of fishing along the Gulf over for perhaps years, I wonder if our life here is also over. I began to ponder what classes might still be open at LSU and speak with Dad about driving over for a campus tour. He just nods. Dad's body is healing, but his head isn't. He takes on same look he had when Mom got sick. Shoulders always down, head lowered ... and never, never a smile.

Then, on the TV, I watch a man walking the beach... Governor Jindal. He pauses and picks up a tar ball. Behind him, over his shoulder, in a half-foot of water, is a pelican, smeared in oil. The bird, its breathing labored, is unable to lift its big 'ol head.

I recognize the scar. Maggie.

My chest tightens. I drop to my knees, hard. I close my eyes and bring my hands to my mouth, preventing a scream from escaping. I can't even cry. All my tears have already fled the reservoir.

The next day, Maggie's picture appears everywhere – *USA Today, The Times Picayune* – and is shown on every news channel. Not the picture I had in mind for the family album.

This is the day I know I'm moving on.

Maybe I'll spend some time at aunt Ida's with Grandpa. Possibly I'll head off to LSU, or join the Coast Guard. Or I could just—quit.

Yes, quit. Lie down and die. That's how awful I feel. Don't believe it'll get any better tomorrow or any time soon. Hurricane Katrina, then this disaster—it's more than this poor land, our beloved Gulf, and I, can take.

I finish reading Melville's classic. His madman's quest failed, Captain Ahab went down with the ship ... *which, like Satan, would not sink to hell till she had dragged a living part of heaven along with her....*"

Pray the Gulf's way of life doesn't descend into hell. My Dad deserves a better fate than Ahab.

# The Oldest Debt

As the ambulance screamed into the yard, its siren winding down, the beams from its revolving lights chased each other across the old man's face, up the brick wall and across the windows. They flashed red streaks across the white clapboard of the house across the street, and then danced diagonally down the chain link fence, intermittently coloring each diamond strand of galvanized wire. Then they slipped from the fence, resuming their race over the sidewalk, down the curb, and across the dirt street once again.

In the next instant, the ambulance seemed to explode, and the three paramedics were out in an instant, already pulling on plastic gloves. Their boots kicked up a dust cloud that mixed with the dust from the ambulance and hovered over the barren yard, then settled on the old man's clothing.

A paramedic grabbed the old man by the shoulders and peered into his eyes. The revolving lights flashed over the back of the paramedic's head, momentarily lighting his close-cropped blond hair with a surrealistic pinkish hue. "I'm Mike. I'm here to help you, okay? Where's the victim? Are you a relative? Sir?"

Mike's colleagues slammed open the back door of the ambulance and reached inside for their equipment.

The old man nodded. "Relative... yes. My name?" He straightened just a bit and met the young paramedic's gaze. His eyebrows arched. "I am Raphael... Raphael Cordones." He motioned toward the house. "She... my wife—"

Maintaining his grip on the old man's shoulders, the paramedic leaned forward and looked intensely at him. "Sir—Mr. Cordones— is she in the house?"

Raphael's slight frame sagged and he trembled, then nodded. "Inside, yes... but I... I do not know yet how I might pay, and—"

Mike looked over his shoulder and yelled, "In the house!" Then he released Raphael and raced for the front door.

The old man slowly turned his five-foot frame and limped toward the house, dust still settling in the creases of his worn khaki trousers and shirt. The lights continued to race across the yard, up the brick wall and across the windows, alternately illuminating his path.

By the time Raphael stepped onto the porch, the paramedic had already shoved aside the battered oak coffee table and was kneeling beside the couch, his stethoscope over his neck. An elderly woman lay before him, supine and still.

Raphael touched him on the shoulder. "Excuse me, Sir. I need to know—"

The other two paramedics rushed through the door with the gurney. One, a young Latino woman, placed her hands on Raphael's shoulders and gently but insistently moved him aside, then knelt alongside the first paramedic. "How's she doin', Mike?"

"Not good, Maria. She's still here, though. Wanna get a saline IV started for me?"

"Sure." With the precision and easy efficiency that comes only with endless practice, the young woman reached into her kit. She stood and hooked a bag of saline solution to the hook on the portable hanger that protruded over the head of the gurney. She reached into the kit again, removing a sealed plastic bag full of tubing and hooked it to the bag.

Raphael stared for a long moment at his wife of over sixty years. His eyes harbored sorrow, but they also held a look that was something akin to relief. Eventually he tore his gaze away from her and shook his head. He turned to look at the third paramedic, Charlie, a tall, slim young black man with glasses who remained near the gurney just inside the front door. He was watching as Maria hooked up the saline drip. "Think that'll do it. Looks good, Maria."

"Thanks, Charlie."

As Raphael shuffled toward them, Maria brushed past him on her way back to the couch, where she resumed her position near Mike. "Good veins?"

He shook his head. "Not so much."

Maria reached into her kit a third time and pulled out a small package containing a butterfly needle, then took out a few alcohol swabs and a short roll of white tape.

Raphael glanced in her direction, then touched Charlie's arm lightly. "Sir? I'm not sure how I can pay, and—"

Charlie smiled sympathetically. He put one hand on Raphael's shoulder. It felt bony beneath his hand. The old man's suspender strap was faded and all but threadbare, the almost limp elastic showing through in several spots. The paramedic shook his head. "You don't owe us anything, Sir. Nothing at all. She's your wife, right? How long has she been down?"

Raphael looked at him. "She... yes, she's my wife...." He shook his head. "No, no money... but I mean, I will pay." He seemed to drift into his own thoughts. "Of course I will.... I must.... I just do not know—"

"It'll be all right, Sir. You just hang here with me and let my friends help her. It'll be all right." He bent slightly to peer into Raphael's eyes. "Do you know how long she's been down? Sir?"

Raphael nodded and glanced at the couch, then back to Charlie. "She was just so sick.... I... maybe ten minutes, I think... maybe. She's been there about ten minutes. I did not know who to call, what to do.... how to pay.... I'm just not sure yet how I can—"

Mike looked over his shoulder. "Okay Charlie. Let's get her on the gurney."

Charlie guided Raphael to the overstuffed easy chair on the other side of the living room. "Wait here, Sir. It'll be all right." As Raphael grasped the arms of the chair and gingerly sat, Charlie turned away and pulled the coffee table farther into the room. Maria helped Mike position the gurney alongside the couch.

Mike leaned over the arm of the couch and slipped one arm under the old woman's frail left shoulder. Maria slipped both arms under her right shoulder, and Charlie gently grasped her legs just above her ankles. Mike looked up. "On my count: one... two... *three*."

As they lifted the woman from the couch and placed her as gently as possible on the gurney, Raphael struggled to his feet. Maria busied herself with finding a viable vein in the back of the woman's hand. She swabbed the area, easily inserted the butterfly needle, taped it to the back of her hand, and attached the tubing for the saline drip.

Raphael slowly limped across the floor toward the paramedics. "Sir? I really need to know—"

Just then a patrol car pulled up and two officers stepped out and crossed the yard, the lights from their car joining the lights from the ambulance in the haunting race up the brick wall and across the windows. Their shoes sounded loudly on the hollow wooden porch before the screen door creaked and they walked in. "What you got, Mike?"

"Stroke, I think. Unstable as hell. She must be 80 though, if she's a day." He saw Raphael coming and put up one hand, palm out. "Sir, you have to stay back now." He looked at the cop again. "You guys handle the husband for us?"

The younger officer nodded. "Sure." He took the old man's arm and guided him gently back toward the overstuffed chair in the opposite corner of the room. "Sir? What's your name?"

"Raphael... I am Raphael Cordones. Officer, I need to know—"

"Okay, Mr. Cordones. This lady is your wife?" Raphael thought the officer spoke louder and more carefully than was necessary. "You been married quite awhile?"

Raphael glanced toward the couch, toward where the woman he'd loved his entire life had lain only moments earlier, and nodded slowly, as if momentarily lost in thought. He looked at the officer oddly, as if wondering whether to trust him. "She was just so sick. I... she has been sick before, but not like this. So much pain this time... too much pain. And she wanted... said she wanted... said she needed...."

As the paramedics pushed the gurney through the doorway behind the officer, the spring on the screen door strained again, protesting as the door itself slapped hard against the clapboard wall. When they proceeded off the porch and across the yard, the door slammed back against the door jamb.

Now the older officer approached Raphael. "Sir, it's all right now. The paramedics will take good care of her. You want a ride to the hospital?"

Raphael seemed relieved to speak with the older officer. "Oh, no.... No, there's no need." His eyes teared. "Sixty-two years we were together. I loved her. But I must stay here. Officer, what I need to know is how to pay. I do not know how I can—"

At the sound of the gurney sliding into the ambulance, the officer interrupted him. "Sir, you want to ride down with her in the ambulance? You can ride down with her if you like, right there in the ambulance."

Raphael stared at him, deep worry lines furrowing his brow.

Mike's voice drifted in from the outside. "Okay, let's roll. Oh damn! She's crashing!"

The older officer started, as if pinched. He glanced at the other officer. "Stay here, Rob. I'll make the run." Then he was out the door speaking to the paramedics. "Follow me to County, Mike. Seven minutes, max. I'll block Main."

Raphael tried again with the younger officer. "Officer, I must pay.... How can I possibly pay when—"

The young man put his hands gently on Raphael's shoulders. "Sir—Mr. Cordones—she'll be all right. They'll have her at County in about ten minutes."

The old man nodded, again seemingly lost in thought. "Ten minutes... ten minutes...." He turned and began to limp across the room. When he reached the screen door, he stared into the darkness, the lights no longer racing across the yard, having sped out into eternity. The sound of the sirens filtered through the heavy night air, but grew more and more distant as he listened.

*These men do not understand,* Raphael thought. *She was sick before, but never like this... never in such pain. And I must pay. They don't understand. She said she wanted the pills, needed them. The special pills, all of them. I do owe. It is the oldest debt of all. I must pay.*

"Mr. Cordones, are you sure you don't want to go to the hospital? When my partner comes back, we could take you."

Raphael turned to look at the officer and sighed. *They just don't listen. They just don't understand. If only there were another way for me to pay....* He nodded. "Yes... yes, perhaps I will go. She will need her rosary." He limped toward the bedroom, his mind racing. "I will get some things."

As he stepped into the bedroom, he closed the door softly, turning the lock in the center of the door knob. He couldn't help wondering what might happen to the younger officer. *I hope he will be all right... it is not his fault.*

When Raphael shut the bedroom door behind him, the young officer took a seat in the overstuffed chair and picked up a dog-eared copy of *Time* magazine from the coffee table. He was turning to an article on the overall reduction in violent crime in the nation's capitol when another article caught his eye: *The Oldest Debt: Cain and Abel.* The subtitle read *Responsibility—Are We Our Brother's Keeper?* The author of the article had taken an unusual stance. Perhaps Cain had slain Abel not in a jealous rage, the author theorized, but as an act of love. *Ridiculous,* he thought, but he found the idea intriguing.

Several paragraphs into the article the author noted the increasing popularity of human euthanasia among the nation's elderly, those members of what Brokaw called The Greatest Generation who had married young and remained married most of their lives. *Sixty-two years, Mr. Cordones said,* he thought. Then he remembered the old man had also used the past tense: *I loved her.* As goosebumps crept up his arms, he all but leapt from the chair and raced across the living room, barking his shin on the coffee table. When he tried the bedroom door knob, it wouldn't turn. He tapped lightly on the door. "Sir—Mr. Cordones—are you all right?"

Raphael sat quietly on the edge of his bed, his feet on the floor and a faraway look in his eyes. *The pills were too many. I knew... she knew... they were just too many. She was in such pain.*

The officer tapped harder on the door. "Sir? Mr. Cordones?"

Raphael placed his trembling hands together, touched them to his chin, then raised them toward the ceiling. *Dios, Dios... forgive this weak human frame. I knew the pills were too many. But she hurt. Ah Dios, how she hurt! But I knew. I knew....*

He lowered his hands, resting one on each side of him on the mattress, then leaned forward and reached for the drawer on the nightstand. He pulled a pistol from the bureau drawer and his trembling hands stilled.

The officer banged on the door. "Mr. Cordones!"

Down the block, more sirens sounded, joining the racing lights to form a wailing red sound, speeding into eternity.

**BETH BLACK**
# How You Play the Game

"Okay, everyone. Texas Hold'em. I've got the dealer button, and you know the drill. Get ready to post your blinds."

Sam shuffled all fifty-two. "Johnny, you're up for first blind. What do you have?"

"Oh, how about an acrostic?" He tossed it into the center of the table.

The others winced. Someone called out, "It doesn't spell out *MOMMY*, does it?"

"Where's the *poet*? Show him! Show him!"

"Yeah, yeah, Johnny. We all know you're here." Sam turned to the next player and said, "Okay, Isaac, your turn. Second blind. Let's get this game off the ground."

"Acrostic, eh? Pretty cheap, I think." Isaac's heavily accented voice curled like steam in a public bath. He checked his stack, withdrawing one. "I'm in for a subplot."

Sam turned to the next man in the circle. He was about to address him when the gentleman interrupted. " – I am not an insect! Please stop calling me that. You know how to say *Anton*. Maybe you can't spell it?" His smile hinted of vinegar. He snapped up the cards as they were dealt.

Sam smirked. "Sure, I can spell *Anton*. Who can't? It's just that *Ants* seems to fit you so much better."

A card hung mid-air as Sam paused to check the reaction on Ants' face. This was not without reward.

"Come on, gentlemen," Johnny reprimanded them. "Keep it going. I have a hot metonymy burning a hole in my purse."

"Not for long, my friend," replied Isaac. He scanned his opponents with one eye.

Deftly, Sam gave each player his private two. All the cards were dealt. Eyes darted from cards to other eyes. Grown men tried to look serious, or failing that ... unreadable, or failing that ... unimaginable.

Sam pushed back his dealer's cap and tugged at one of his rolled-up sleeves. The bands were obviously a little too tight. Either that, or he was sneaking murderers out from under his upper sleeves. He dealt *The Flop*.

Ants observed the three community cards now on the table and swore under his breath. "Dreadful!  You always do this to me!"

A late player darted in through the glass door and scrambled into his seat.  "Sorry, gentlemen," he said. "We've been moving again. The invitation didn't find me right away."

"Nobody I know moves around like you, Jimmy." Joe cocked his head and eyed him. "Where were you this time?  I don't suppose you've gone to...Africa?"

Jimmy sighed. "No, you can rest easy, Joe.  Not everyone goes to the Dark Continent."

"That's good. You wouldn't want to go there.  The horror! The horror!"

Once more, Jimmy sighed. "Calm down!  We're back in Italy." They examined each other. He pressed it. "Really."

"Just deal him in," said Leo.

"Anything you say." With that, Sam pulled two cards from the remaining deck for Jimmy.  "It'll cost you, though."

"Sure, pal."  Jimmy reached into his vest pocket and pulled out an undecipherable literary reference.  He threw it into the pot.

Joe sniffed at it. "Awe, c'mon!  Nobody likes those!"

"Yeah, but they're valuable, and certainly something you'd never see if I weren't in the game." Jimmy stared him down.

"Okay, fine.  But, that means war," Joe snapped, "And I've got just the framed narrative to do it."

"Come, now Connie. Let's not get testy," said Sam.

"Don't call me that...*Sammy*."

"Ouch.  Fine."

Johnny broke the tension by asking, "Okay, whose bet is it?  If it's mine...all aboard – an alliteration!" And he angled it in.

Chuck sneaked a peek at Ari's raised eyebrows – a sure *tell*. Covering his glee, he sniffed and cleared his throat. "I'll see you and raise you a holiday moral."

There was a clanging knock on the glass door of the casino's card game room.  The men peered through the pane.

"Oh, hell. Who invited her? I said no women, little or otherwise," Ari said, his voice roaring.

"Don't get your unities in a knot. Louisa knows this is a men's game. Just smile and wave and keep playing," Sam said, smiling and waving and then pushing his cards around in his hand.

The attendant, a burly guy named Gogol, positioned himself at the door. He seized the knob.

Louisa tried to open the door, but the struggle went to Gogol. Finally giving in, Louisa waved back with what looked like an unrequited love in one hand and a dying child in the other.

"Christ! What histrionics! Let's have the attendant shoo her away." Ants sneered.

Ari snorted. "Yes, I came here to play cards, not be bullied by some liberated female."

No sooner had Ari belittled women, than Louisa, apparently in response, crumpled up her dying child and her unrequited love, stuffed them into her purse, stuck out her tongue at the players and strode away.

"Okay, now we can play." Ari stole a glimpse of the others' pursed their lips then grinned. "I'll bet a Greek tragedy."

Everyone groaned.

Sam picked up his cigar, lit it, and took a long drag, puffing grey-white smoke above the table. It swirled and rose into the glare of the Tiffany style chandelier. He signaled to Jimmy. "You want to do something about this, now that you're in?" he asked.

Jimmy heaved in his bet. "Sure, I'll see yours and raise you a Greek tragedy...*set in modern day.*"

More groans.

Ants plunked down a musical comedy. A few eyebrows went up. "It was a gift," he explained.

"Some of the men nodded. Johnny said, "Reminds me of the time someone gave me a Hallmark card. What the hell can you do with that?"

The others sniggered.

"Your turn, Johnny. You gonna laugh all day or you gonna play?" Jimmy grew impatient. Holding an unreadable stance was, after all, tedious.

Johnny surreptitiously surveyed the others. "Nope. I think I'll pass."

With a shrug, Isaac unloaded some similes and Sam followed with a couple of anachronisms yanked from a secret compartment in the pocket watch made especially for him in a Connecticut factory.

"Okay, Leo. It's up to you." Sam puffed again. More smoke swirled.

Leo, who had been studying his cards asked, "Where is the vodka? This is a thirsty man's game."

Gogol sprang into action and a bottle of vodka was immediately opened and poured for all.

Isaac raised his glass. "L'Chaim!" He emptied it, turned it over, and slapped it onto the table.

"*Za vashe zdorovye!*" Leo answered, and did the same with his glass. More was poured while he placed his bet. "I'll see all of you and raise you a three-act play."

"What? Only three? I think he's holding back," Ari said.

"It's not for you to say!" Leo bellowed.

Ants nodded hastily in agreement.

Ari was not deterred. "Oh, yeah? Well, I have a five-act play that says you're full of shit!" He dragged it across the table to the center pot, which was now gaining a respectable size.

Sam raised his cigar. "Now, gentlemen. We need to go in order. First –"

He was interrupted. A loud knock drew everyone's attention to the glass door.

"Oh, for Pete's sake!" Ants huffed.

Louisa's face, lustrous with anger, glowered through the glass. Beside her stood the general manager of the casino. The attendant quickly retreated from the door, and they entered the room.

"I'm sorry to intrude, gentlemen."

Ari warmed up his retort. "Well, you are –"

"– Not at all, sir," Sam intervened. "What can we do for you?"

"You know it's against the law to discriminate here. We could lose an entire *How-To-Play* book over this. You really have to open your game."

Isaac chimed in. "Book Schmook."

"I think this game is about to end," Jimmy yelled, "And I only just arrived!"

Each man grumbled and shifted uncomfortably in his seat.

"Let's all just calm down, shall we?" said Chuck. "Look, if the little lady wants to play with us, I say we let her in. We can still have the best of times, not the worst. Let's use our wisdom here, and not be foolish. I believe, if you're not incredulous, that this can be a lighthearted game, unless the darkness of your souls keeps these women out. Let them spring, hopeful, into this wintry room without despair...and, we'll have everything before us (all they own, anyway). Maybe I'll go to heaven, although I suspect *you're* all going to –"

Jimmy cut him off. "– Chuck! Put up or shut up."

"I believe I already did," he replied. After an emphatic pause, he added, "We're short two spots anyway."

Louisa snagged a seat. "Not for long," she said. "I called Dottie."

The men stared around the table at each other.

Sam scratched the back of his neck. "I suppose she'll be wearing glasses."

"You are so predictable, Sam." Jimmy picked up his hand.

Sam answered with a long drag puffed in Jimmy's direction.

"Normally I would love to have both women join us, but actually, we're saving a spot. Bill's coming, isn't he?" Johnny asked.

Joe gaped. "I hope Bill isn't coming. Those iambic pentameters are so hard to unload these days. Just try 'em at Sears." He rearranged his hand.

"When did Bill ever lose to you?" Johnny asked, giving him the eye.

"Once or twice. It happened." He paused, and glanced around. "It could happen, y'know." Joe turned his attention fiercely to his cards.

"Yeah, sure," said Isaac. "So, Louisa, put in your dead child and let's move on."

"Right, let's do. *The Turn.*" Sam placed a fourth card face up on the table. He clucked his tongue at the results.

Everyone studied their cards. Betting resumed around the table, and Louisa pleasantly surprised the gentlemen by pulling an intelligent antagonist from her purse.

Dottie arrived and took her seat. Of course, she wore glasses. The men barely noticed her. She threw in a clever couplet and three metaphors, then snatched up two cards from Sam.

The attendant rummaged through his serving cart, gradually proffering chocolates to the ladies.

"I could use some liquor," posed Dottie.

He complied...quicker.

Dottie swung her glass in the air and sang, ""Here's to those who wish us well, and those that don't may go to hell!" She paused, adding, "Okay, so I borrowed it. I needed all of mine for the game." She laughed, finished her drink in one gulp, and smacked the glass down hard. When she removed her eyeglasses, the men were finally impressed.

Leo winked at her. "What are you doing later?"

She sniffed at him. "Aren't you married?"

"So?"

"No!" She turned back to her cards. Social conventions may not have been her favorite part of life, but Dottie had no intention of battling them over a guy with *that* nose.

Sam dealt *The River*. Five cards blinked back at everyone.

Chuck placed his bet, but Sam smelled a rat. He scooped it out of the pile and pressed it between his teeth. "Hey! I'm a'callin' your bluff, pal!"

"Uh-oh. This ought to separate the men from the boys," whispered Louisa to Dottie.

Sam held up Chuck's bet. "Bet your bottom dollar...it's a *cliché*!"

All eyes turned on Chuck. He curled his lip. "I guess the writing's on the wall."

"And you are *such* a moralist!" cried Jimmy.

"Thank you!" Chuck guffawed.

The game took a hard turn for Louisa. "It's so dreadful to be poor! Christmas won't be Christmas without any presents," she grumbled, lying on the rug. The attendant revived her with a suck of pickled lime...a sprinkle of salt and a shot of tequila. Isaac, and Joe suffered, as well. All three folded when the betting reached climactic proportions.

It wasn't much easier for the others. Leo lost several trains, including one train of thought. Dottie stayed in the game, but placed her bets with some caution. The pot even looked a bit rich for Chuck, despite all his affluent adjectives, and he folded. At length, only a few players remained.

Sam grinned with his usual mischief in mind. The others hated him for it, and Ari threatened to bring out a rulebook. Johnny convinced him to sit back and relax. "No use growing irritated over a few doubts," he counseled.

"Enjoy the game," Leo said, dropping his cards in disgust. "What else is it for but some fun, anyway?" Leo was always unhappy in his own way. He couldn't help but smile.

"Well, I for one always learn something from this," said Johnny, "like knowing when to hold'em, and when to fold'em, and when to run away." He toyed with his few polysyndetons, whistling at the fact that he'd folded early enough to keep them.

Scowling, Dottie finally folded.

Ants stared at Sam, trying to read those lips. His Cheshire grin stretched wide enough to explain the cards on the table, but not those in his hand. Ants demanded a *Showdown*.

Jimmy placed his cards face down, as well. "You sure you want to do that? Last time, I lost an entire epic. Never again."

Jimmy's argument was like a fiend at Ants' throat. The game was hopelessly lost. "Okay, Sam. We all fold. So, c'mon, show us what you have." He attempted to wave his hand in Sam's disarming manner. He failed.

"I don't have to do that. You all know it, as well. I'm surprised you even ask."

Ari nodded. "Game over."

Ants grumbled that only entropy came easy.

Everyone pulled away from the table.

"You want to go play the slots, Joe?" Jimmy said, "I've got some loose character traits weighing down my pockets."

"Yeah, sure. Can I swap you a few for a setting?"

"What kind?" Jimmy asked.

"Oh, I think...a woods. Maybe a, um, haunted castle."

Jimmy frowned at him. "You crook. Okay, yeah...sure. Fine." They opened the game room door as he dug into his pocket.

"Wait!" Sam waved to the others. "Don't go just yet."

"Oh?" Jimmy swung back to him. "You just can't drop a chance to show off, can you?"

Ari shook with laughter.

Chuck chuckled and rubbed his cold arms. "It's a fact, sir, that I'm not interested." He always tried to stick to the facts, even during such hard times.

Isaac eyed Sam. "Jesus! What a ham. So? What do you have?" His Euro accent grew thicker and clouded the room even more.

Sam beamed like a father who was watching his child win a spelling bee. He laid his two cards on the table face down. "Simple, my friends. You want to see, pay up *big time*."

The others groaned.

"It's probably not worth it," warned Louisa.

"Oh, but it is," said Sam, laughing. "More than a river full of books."

"Well, I don't believe you," said Louisa.

"I always tell the truth, mainly," said Sam with forged solemnity and a wink at Dottie.

Johnny searched his pockets. "All I have are these." He jangled his few polysyndetons heartily, trying to force more noise out of them.

Sam shook his head, grinning and glinting and smirking at him.

Johnny winced. "Then, I believe I'm negatively capable in that regard."

"Suit yourself. Not everyone needs a mystery solved," replied Sam.

Dottie took the bait. She dropped herself into the seat left vacant by Johnny. "Trapped like a trap in a trap," she sighed.

Sam laughed. "You and your anaphoras! That won't do it."

"Oh, yeah? Just watch me." She smirked at him lustily.

"The lady has balls, gentlemen!" Then, he turned to her and said, "Okay, what do you *really* have? Otherwise, you'll never see these." He drummed his fingers on the cards.

Dottie's face lit up more than Sam's. She leaned in close to him and whispered, "Oh, I want to see. I want to see very much, my friend." She reached down to her shoe and pulled something from inside the heel. With care and pleasure she unfolded it. "It's the last thing I've got," she said.

Dottie drew a breath, raised the treasure over her head, and then in a grand gesture, plunked it down. Clapping her hands together, she declared, "A perfect ending!"

## E. SCOTT MENTER

# Dolphinarium

What if it had rained?

Anya hated the rain. In the old country, the rain would fall often during the hot, sticky summer, continuing into the autumn. On the sunny days, Tatiana and I would trot along behind our only daughter as she raced down one block and up the next until we reached the park. There, like a bumblebee, Anya would zip from tree to flower to lake's edge, then halt, still as marble, suddenly entranced by a ladybug, or a kitten, or a perfectly smooth stone. We would find a bench or a rock to sit on, far enough not to intrude on her play, close enough to rush to her if she needed us.

By November, the clouds would freeze, the hard cold and heavy snow unrelenting until spring. Anya had real fur-lined mittens, a thick down jacket that used to be Tatiana's, and a fur cap that had cost a week's pay. Tatiana inspected her carefully each morning before school, fussing over every button and zipper, making sure the mittens were snug—but not too snug—and the socks dry, with no holes. Only then would we set out for the ugly cinderblock school Tatiana had once attended, the school from which she had been expelled soon after her parents applied for exit visas.

Now, with the Communists gone, we were no longer prevented from leaving as Tatiana's family had been. I was willing to consider the idea of emigration, but Tatiana was impatient. Finally, one day as we trudged through the snow, she stepped in front of me. She took my hands in hers, her green eyes looking directly into mine. "Alexei, it is time."

"Time? Time for what?"

"Time to go, Alexei. To leave this place."

"We've talked about this, *maya krasaveetsa.*"

"Yes. We have talked. But Anya is six years old—we have talked long enough. I do not want her growing up here. The poverty, the corruption, the drunken thugs on the street—there is no future here. Especially for us."

"Tatiana..."

"You know it is true. It is dangerous here for us."

"No more so than for anybody else."

She shook her head and smiled softly. The memory of her life as a refusenik–her father's imprisonment, her mother's heartbreak–haunted her eyes. "You don't know, Alexei. These people–they hate us. You see yourself as Russian, but they do not. To them, you are *yevrei*. As am I. As is Anya."

I was unconvinced. However, for my wife and daughter, I would have moved to the South Pole.

That spring, we emigrated to Israel. Throughout the decade that followed, we remained outsiders of a sort. Though very comfortable in our enclave, we remained *olim hadashim*, immigrants, never truly integrated into mainstream society. We rarely had to rely on our heavily accented Hebrew. Our friends and neighbors were Russian, TV programs were either in Russian or were subtitled, and even our tax forms spelled it out in Russian.

Anya, however, grew up an Israeli, a real *sabra*. She spoke rapid-fire Hebrew and was immersed in Israeli popular culture. In this country where a former refusenik had become a cabinet minister, where a million of my countrymen had been absorbed, if not always welcomed, my daughter found acceptance and happiness. Not that there weren't difficult moments, as when Anya wanted her mother's help preparing for a party at school. "Ima, would you help me sew a Purim costume? I want to be a belly dancer."

"Anna Alexova! A belly dancer? What would people think?"

Anya rolled her eyes, a very Israeli gesture. "They will think I'm wearing a Purim costume, like everybody else."

"What, you can't go as Queen Esther?"

"Oy, Ima. It's 2001. You think people still dress as characters from the Megillah for Purim?"

Tatiana's features softened. "I wouldn't know, Anushka. When I was little, we did not wear Purim costumes. If we had, we would have been expelled from school, forced to leave our apartment, perhaps even arrested."

Anya was silent for a moment. We expected further bargaining, or perhaps another eye-roll. Instead, she moved to Tatiana, embraced her tightly, and leaned her head on her shoulder. "I'm sorry, Ima. I am."

Tatiana hugged her, peering at me over Anya's shoulder with wet eyes. Anya had learned in school about the struggles of Soviet Jewry, and we'd answered whatever questions she'd asked about our lives. She even retained some dim memories of the old country. But until that moment, she hadn't fully absorbed what it had been like for us, Jewish children in a land Jews were considered traitors, outcasts.

Anya's world could hardly have been more different. She was self-assured, beautiful, in every way a typical Western teenager. She loved to spend time with her friends, listen to music, go to the movies, or shop at one of the new malls that seemed to keep appearing out of nowhere.

Still, we hesitated on that warm Friday evening in June when she asked if she could go to a beachside disco with her friends. "This is not something we do on Shabbat, Anuskha."

"We don't do anything on Shabbat, Ima. We're not religious, so what does it matter? All my friends are going."

"When I was a girl, we—"

"Yes, I know, Ima. When you were a girl, you stayed home every evening and played chess while discussing politics and mathematics over a plate of borscht. So thank you again for moving here, where I don't have to spend every night sitting at home. Can I go please?"

"Aleksei, talk to her."

Anya turned her big green eyes to me. "Abba, all my friends will be there."

"So you mentioned."

"So nu? What's the problem?"

"Well, we think you are too young to be going out dancing unchaperoned."

"Yael's parents are letting her go. Also Irina's."

"I see. And maybe Ilya, as well?"

Anya blushed. The older brother of Anya's best friend Irina, Ilya was on leave from the Army. The two of them had visited the previous day. Tatiana and I had grown up far away and in a very different time, but some things are universal, and the face of a teen-aged girl with a crush is one of them.

Anya answered quietly, her expression briefly revealing the shy schoolgirl within: "Yes, Ilya too."

I glanced at Tatiana. She wasn't going to like this. "OK, motek. You call me every hour. If you miss one call, you will not leave this apartment for a year."

Anya squealed, hugging me, then her mother, before racing upstairs to get ready. Tatiana closed her eyes, shook her head, and left the room without a word.

An hour later, Anya hugged us again and ran out the door with Yael, Irina, and Ilya, who had stopped by to collect her. Tatiana and I stayed behind to do what parents of teenagers around the world do: sit on the couch and wait for her to return.

If only it had rained. Anya hated the rain. She might have stayed home.

As midnight approached, Anya was standing among dozens of other kids, some as young as 14, on the boardwalk outside the dance club. The sea was inky black, the air warm and redolent of salt. She was supposed to have called home long before, but she and her friends were savoring their youth, joking, teasing, "making life", as the Israelis say. They paid no attention to the time, or to the stranger among them.

The intruder, a Palestinian Arab, was dressed as a religious Jew. He was on a mission, but there was no hurry: paradise would wait a few more moments. He watched the children for a while, even chatted with some, before doing what he came there to do.

The explosive vest was laden with bolts and ball bearings that ripped through the flesh of the nearby children as its force tore their bodies apart. A sudden cloudburst of blood and tissue showered the boardwalk, soaking the survivors, pelting them with scraps of the bone and sinew of their classmates, their girlfriends, their brothers and sisters.

Their screams rose above the cry of the sirens as rescue workers descended on the scene.

One hot, dry day extends into the next. Tatiana rarely speaks, her silence settling hard onto my already unbearable guilt. I wander the apartment at night, tormented by questions with no answers.

When I finally sleep, Anya appears to me in my dreams. She is covered in blood. "Now, Abba," she says, "now you are truly an Israeli."

**LEONARD FREDERICK**

# THE HUMMINGBIRD
## (A Modern Telling of A Mayan Tale)

Tzunuum, the hummingbird, was created by the Great Spirit as a tiny, delicate bird with extraordinary flying ability. She was the only bird in the kingdom who could fly backwards and who could hover in one spot for several seconds. The hummingbird was very plain. Her feathers had no bright colors, yet she didn't mind. Tzunuum took pride in her flying skill and was happy with her life despite her looks. When it came time to be married, Tzunuum found that she had neither a wedding gown nor a necklace.

She was so disappointed and sad that some of her best friends decided to surprise her by creating a wedding dress and jewelry. Ya, the vermilion-crowned flycatcher, wore a gay crimson ring of feathers around his throat. He decided to use it as his gift. So he tucked a few red plumes in his crown and gave the rest to the hummingbird for her necklace. Uchilchil, the bluebird, generously donated several blue feathers for her gown. The vain motmot, not to be outdone, offered more turquoise blue and emerald green. The cardinal, likewise, gave some red ones. Yuyum, the oriole, an excellent tailor as well as an engineer, sewed up all the plumage into an exquisite wedding gown for the little hummingbird. Ah-leum, the spider, crept up with a fragile web woven of shiny gossamer threads for her veil. She helped Mrs. Yuyum weave intricate designs into the dress. Canac, the honeybee, heard about the wedding and told all his friends who knew and liked the hummingbird. They brought much honey and nectar for the reception and hundreds of blossoms that were Tzunuum's favorites. The Azar tree dropped a carpet of petals over the ground where the ceremony would take place. She offered to let Tzunuum and her groom spend their honeymoon in her branches. Pakal, the orange tree, put out sweet-smelling blossoms, as did Nicte, the plumeria vine. Haaz (the banana bush), Op the custard apple tree) and Pichi and Put (the guava and papaya bushes) made certain that their fruits were ripe so the wedding guests would find

winter / spring 2011

delicious refreshments. And, finally, a large band of butterflies in all colors arrived to dance and flutter gaily around the hummingbird's wedding site.

When the wedding day arrived, Tzunuum was so surprised, happy and grateful that she could barely twitter her vows. The Great Spirit so admired her humble, honest soul that he sent word down with his messenger, Cozumel, the swallow, that the hummingbird could wear her wedding gown for the rest of her life. To this day, she has.

How did the humility of one long-ago hummingbird cause its descendants to sport brilliant colors?

contributor bios

# CONTRIBUTOR BIOS

DAVID AMRAM has composed more than 100 orchestral and chamber music works and written many scores for Broadway theater and film, including: the classic scores for the films *Splendor in the Grass* and *The Manchurian Candidate*; two operas; and the score for the landmark 1959 documentary *Pull My Daisy*, narrated by novelist Jack Kerouac. He is also the author of three books: *Vibrations*, an autobiography; *Offbeat: Collaborating with Kerouac*, a memoir; and *Upbeat: Nine Lives of a Musical Cat.* He has collaborated with Leonard Bernstein, Dizzy Gillespie, Langston Hughes, Dustin Hoffman, Willie Nelson, Thelonious Monk, Odetta, Elia Kazan, Arthur Miller, Charles Mingus, Lionel Hampton, Johnny Depp and Tito Puente.

LINDA ENGEL AMUNDSON has worked in sales, corporate spying, the hospitality industry and accounting. She is an art jewelry designer, fond of repurposed objects and found industrial parts. Linda lives in the San Diego area with her small blind dog and husband. Her work has appeared in *Thunderclap Magazine* and the *San Diego Poetry Annual.*

RYKA AOKI has an MFA in Creative Writing from Cornell University, where she won a University Award from the Academy of American Poets. The California State Senate honored her for creating Trans/Giving, LA's only art/performance series dedicated to trans*, genderqueer, and intersex artists. Two of her compositions were adopted by the American Association of Hiroshima-Nagasaki A-Bomb Survivors as its "Songs of Peace." In 2010, she won the RADAR's Eli Coppola Poetry Chapbook Competition (Incognito Press). Her poems have appeared in the *Jacaranda Review*, *Asian American Literary Review, Lodestar Quarterly, Grand Street*, and the *Southern Poetry Review*.

BETH BLACK graduated from UC Irvine, where she received a grant to write a collection of short stories. Her staff creative writer at Toastmasters International requires her to write and edit in any genre – nonfiction, fiction, comedy, comics, Web, journalism, etc. She's also an Associate Editor of the *Toastmaster* magazine, reaching 260,000 readers in 113 countries. Nominated for a Pushcart Prize a few years ago, Beth continues freelance writing for literary magazines and has several projects in progress.

MICHAEL BLAKE is back with an excerpt from his latest novel, *Into the Stars.* He is the author of *Dances With Wolves,* the 1986 novel whose screenplay (which he also wrote) led to one of the most popular movies in history, and earned him the 1991 Academy Award. Based in southeastern Arizona, he's written six other books, including *Airman Mortensen* (1991), *Marching to Valhalla* (1997), *The Holy Road* (2001), *Indian Yell* (2006), *Twelve the King* (2009) and his 2002 autobiography, *Like a Running Dog.* Michael has won many awards, including the Environmental Media Award, Golden Quill, American Library Association award and Eleanor Roosevelt award.

MARTE BROEHM's poetry has previously appeared in *Pedestal Magazine, Perigee Literature for the Arts, The Magee Park Poets Anthology, San Diego Poetry Annual, Arsenic Lobster*, and elsewhere. Her chapbook is entitled *Marginalia In Bloom*. Local art galleries exhibit her watercolors and mixed media. A piece of creative nonfiction will appear in Spring 2011 in *The Los Angeles Review*.

GAIL BORNFIELD is a Tucson, Ariz.-based educator, fiction writer, the author of five educational books and the author of *Tampei,* a middle-grades novel currently being shopped for publication. She has published numerous articles and a five-book series to assist teachers with instruction. Her flash fiction, short stories, essays and poems have appeared in numerous publications.

ANGELEE DEODHAR is a haiku poet and artist from India. Her haiku and haiga have been published internationally in various books, journals and on the Internet. She is a member of several haiku groups worldwide, including the Haiku Society of America, Haiku Society of Canada, and Haiku International Association-Japan, Meguro International Friendship Association-Japan, Evergreen Haiku Society-Japan and the World Haiku Association-Japan.

TRISH DUGGER's poetry appears in *California Quarterly, Spillway, Hayden's Ferry Review* and various other anthologies. Her poem, Spare Parts, was selected for Ted Kooser's web site, http://www.americanlifeinpoetry.com.

DICK EIDEN was raised and attended public schools in Pomona, Calif., went to college at UC Santa Barbara and law school at UCLA in the Sixties, and was caught up in and deeply affected by the social movements of those years, especially the anti-war and civil rights movements. He became an activist lawyer in private practice, mostly in Los Angeles, from 1971 until 1994, when he stopped practicing law to become a full time Dad or "DH" (designated homemaker). He now lives in Vista, California, where he founded Sunset Poets (2001), and is still active with many political and social issues.

LEONARD FREDERICK has been a naturalist since the 1960s, and is admittedly obsessive about sustainability and ecology. Much of his ethos lies in his deep devotion to myths of the native peoples. Currently, his engineering and construction business specializes in green building with recycled steel. He works constantly at home with organic gardening and birds.

MAI LON GITTELSOHN lives in Del Mar where she leads classes of seniors in memoir writing. An elementary school teacher in Del Mar for 23 years, she now enjoys writing in Harry Griswold's poetry workshop and singing with Villa

Musica. Her poems have appeared in the *Patterson Literary Review*, the *Magee Park Poets Anthology*, the *WritingItReal* website and the *San Diego Poetry Annual*. A fifth Chinese daughter, Mai Lon grew up in Berkeley, Calif.

HARRY GRISWOLD grew up in New York State, where "home" has rusted into a shell of its once prosperous self. He holds an MFA degree from Pacific University, is the author of *Camera Obscura* (Wordcraft of Oregon), and has recently published in *Argestes, California Quarterly, Gargoyle, Limestone* and *Many Mountains Moving*. For the past 19 years, he has hosted and facilitated "The Pleasures of Poetry" workshop in North San Diego County.

KATE HARDING is Pushcart Prize nominee in both poetry and fiction. Her poems and stories have been published in numerous magazine including *Redbook, California Quarterly, Poetry International, Earth's Daughters, Compass Rose, Perigee, Limestone Circle, Phoebe*, and the *San Diego Poetry Annual*. Her chapbook, *What Women Do*, was a finalist in the Earth's Daughter's chapbook competition. She was ascreenwriting fellow at the American Film Institute; her movie, *A Berkeley Christmas*, aired on PBS.

THEA IBERALL is a poet and scientist. She has a Master's Degree in Writing (USC) and a Ph.D. in Computational Neuroscience (U MASS). Thea has had over 40 poems published in anthologies and journals, including *Rattle, Spillway,* and *The Southern California Anthology*. She has a poem in *Blood to Remember: American Poets on the Holocaust* (Time Being Books). She was a semifinalist in the Atlanta Review International Poetry Competition and she is featured in the documentary *GV6 THE ODYSSEY: Poets, Passion & Poetry*. As a performance poet, Thea represented Los Angeles at the National Poetry Slams.

CLIFTON KING is a native Californian poet. His work has appeared in anthologies, literary journals and online. His first book of poetry, *Stolen Afternoons,* was published in 2006. He received the *Excellence in Literature Award* from Mira Costa College Friends of the Humanities in 2008 and the *Poetry Award* in 2010 for poems that appeared in their annual publication, *Tidepools*. More of his poetry can be found at cliftonkingpoetry.com

KATHRYN KOPPLE returns to *The Hummingbird Review* as a contributing poet; she was the editor of the premier issue. She is a specialist in Latin American literature. Her translations and essays appear in a variety of literary reviews and anthologies including *These Are Not Sweet Girls, Exact Change Yearbook,* and *The Xul Reader*. She has published original works of poetry in *Contemporary Haibun Online* and *Danse Macabre*. She lives and writes in Philadelphia, Pa.

GARY LAWLESS and his wife Beth live on a lakeside farm in Maine with their two donkeys. They own Gulf of Maine Bookstore and publish Blackberry Books.

Gary has published more than 20 collections of poems, and has given readings in Italy, Slovenia, Latvia, Lithuania, Germany and Cuba. His poetry blog is http://mygrations.blogspot.com.

ISAAC LOMELI is an author, teacher and collegiate wrestling coach. His Santa Ana (CA) College team won the 2005 California junior college title. He is originally from Anaheim, CA, where his memoir *Tales from the Eastside* is set — the story of how he turned to literature to find meaning and purpose and refuse to join a gang. He now lives in San Francisco.

TIMOTHY DEAN MARTIN is a long-time poet, songwriter and the author of the forthcoming novel *Mental Hygiene.* He was a lyricist for recording artists that included David Clayton Thomas (of Blood, Sweat & Tears), the DeFranco Family, Manfred Mann, the Outlaws, Cilla Black and many others. In 1989, he won a CLIO Award for best radio commercial. His work can be found at http://www.timothydeanmartin.com.

E. SCOTT MENTER lives in Southern California and has spent considerable time in Israel. Scott spends his time writing, practicing martial arts, and trying to keep up with his two teen-aged kids and his wife, Jackie. A software entrepreneur by day, Scott transforms into the blogger Writer of Wrongs by night (blog. WriterOfWrongs.net). "Dolphinarium" won the Fall 2010 Hummingbird Review writing contest, co-sponsored by the Southern California Writers Conference.

WILLIAM THOMPSON ONG, an award-winning Madison Avenue creative director, has written and produced hundreds of commercials for national consumer brands like Crest, Scope, and Cheerios. He also co-founded an advertising agency in Philadelphia. Tom is now a full-time novelist, living and writing in Santa Monica, Calif. He is marketing a series of action-adventure novels and is currently writing a semi-biographical work of fiction.

R.D. "DUKE" SKAFF returned to her writing roots in southern California in 2003. This time poetically inspired by her close proximity to the sea. She is published in *American Pen Women Winning Poetry and Haiku, Today's Alternative News, Phantom Seed, San Diego Poetry Annuals* – 2007 through 2010, *Magee Park Poets Anthologies* – 2007 through 2011. Her poetry has also been included in a *Poets Inc. Art Summation Exhibition.*

JOHN VINCENT ROULEAU was raised on the banks of the wild and scenic Saint Croix River in both Wisconsin and Minnesota. His early years were spent pursuing a passion for nature. His first artistic passion was painting, though he's long pursued expression in writing as well. Mr. Rouleau is completing a book of poetry and prose with matched illustrations. John is married with a seven-year-old daughter, and living just outside of San Francisco.

R.T. SEDGWICK is the author of four books of poetry: *Forgotten Woods, Harmony of a Storm, Sand Castles*, and *Circles and Lines*, all published by sedgwickARTcards, Del Mar, Calif., as well as numerous poems published in various anthologies and periodicals. He has attended Harry Griswold's *Pleasures of Poetry* workshop for the last nine years, Idyllwild Summer Arts Poetry in 2005 through 2010 and has participated in a Master Poetry Workshop lead by Dr. Sam Hamod in 2007 and 2009.

HARVEY STANBROUGH's poetry has been nominated for the Pushcart Prize, the National Book Award, the Pulitzer Prize, and the *Inscriptions Magazine* Engraver's Award. He's the author of three poetry collections, *Beyond the Masks, Lessons for a Barren Population* and *Intimations on the Shapes of Things,* his fiction and essays have been widely published, and he's helped thousands of writing students through his Writing the World workshops series and nonfiction books on writing, *Punctuation for Writers* and the award-winning *Writing Realistic Dialogue & Flash Fiction*. He lives and works in southeastern Arizona.

ANDREE STOLTE has read her poems in New York City at Bluestockings, Cornelia Street Café, Fordham University at Lincoln Center, and Casa Italia Zerilli Marimo NYU, and is compiling a collection for publication. She wrote and performed a solo play about First Lady Jacqueline Kennedy titled *Jackie Undressed,* presented at the National Arts Club and various festivals in NYC. Currently, she is speaking a series of essays and poems exploring our relationship to myth and contemporary culture titled *Leaving Camelot Behind*, which can be heard on her you tube channel *HealingAwake*.

D.N. SUTTON has been writing poetry since she was seven — in 1927. She is still being published, her latest contribution coming in the *2011 Magee Park Poets Anthology*. She's the author of three poetry collections: *Love Poems for the Romantic Heart, Death Poems for the Grieving Heart,* and *Psalms for Life Living*. Now 90, her elegant, soulful delivery of poetry makes her a favorite whenever she reads. Three of her plays have been performed and read by poetry troupes, including her newest, *The Living End.*

KELLY THACKER is the author of the romantic suspense novel, *Numberless Dreams.* She owns a court reporting firm and has spent her career in the legal field teaching English, grammar and punctuation to court reporters. She loves incorporating her background into her writing and is hard at work on her second book, a legal thriller involving a court reporter.

NELLY WILLIAMS lives and writes poetry in Puerto Rico.

www.ingramcontent.com/pod-product-compliance
Lightning Source LLC
Chambersburg PA
CBHW030554310325
24155CB00001BA/29